LEGACY OF LOVE

LEGACY OF LOVE

Gifts I Received on the Path of Life

NAN JOHNSON

Legacy of Love: Gifts I Received on the Path of Life
Published by STAGE FOUR PRESS
San Diego, California, U.S.A.

JOHNSON, NAN, Author
LEGACY OF LOVE
NAN JOHNSON

ISBN: 978-0-578-90417-7 (First Edition)
ISBN: 979-8-9862170-0-0 (Second Edition hardcover)
ISBN: 979-8-9862170-1-7 (Second Edition paperback)

BIOGRAPHY & AUTOBIOGRAPHY / Personal Memoirs
BODY, MIND & SPIRIT / Inspiration & Personal Growth

Proceeds from book sales via cvillaphoto.com will support
breast cancer research and treatment organizations.

To my beloved spouse, partner, and soul mate, Connie Villa.
Your love has sustained me, your laughter has uplifted me,
and your wise soul has taught me many things.
Our bond will never be broken.
May you live on in joy and awaken each day
with wonder and gratitude.
May you know that love is all there is.

Contents

INTRODUCTION

Once upon a time there was a young girl, born in 1958, in the midwestern state of Ohio. She considered herself lucky to live in a place where neighbors all knew each other and you could leave your doors unlocked at night. If you forgot your bike outside, it would be exactly where you left it in the morning. As a child she loved the four seasons and the great outdoors. She was blessed with a wonderful family and friends.

What she did not know was that at age twelve, sometime in the summer of 1971, she would receive the greatest, most precious gift of her life. It is through this book that she wants to share with you the essence of this gift and some lessons she learned along the way.

The concept of this book is simple. It is a compilation and collection of my favorite quotes, poems, and personal writings, as well as stories from my life and lessons learned, grouped around twelve themes. At the beginning of every chapter, I introduce the theme. I share my reflections on the topic and where I have seen or experienced it in my life. I also share inspiring stories I have heard that are related to the theme. I then include some quotes, poems, and personal writings. At the end of each chapter you'll find questions to contemplate.

While the concept is simple, the purpose of this book is much deeper. The greatest gift of my life was to awaken to a spiritual path. This happened quite spontaneously on a hot August day at the age of twelve by what I have come to call a moment of Divine Grace. On that particular day, I was reading a spiritual book my great aunt, who our family affectionately called Neppie, had given me for Christmas. The book asked the reader to pause, memorize a short prayer, and repeat it ten times standing in front of a mirror.

With all the sincerity and innocence of a twelve-year-old, I stood in front of my bedroom mirror and repeated the prayer. Out of nowhere, a beautiful, luminous white light descended upon me. It was in me and through me. I was light as a feather. I felt as though I was a foot above the ground. A voice told me the universe is exactly as it should be. It told me not to fear. It also bestowed a great peace in me that I have turned to time and again throughout my life. It started me on my spiritual quest and path.

I cannot think of a greater gift to give you, my loved ones and friends, than a book of inspiration and love. A book of inspiration and love that was born on that summer day. Being on a spiritual path got me through some very tough times in life, especially with cancer and cancer treatments now going on sixteen years. Cancer has been a fierce teacher. No matter how rough those days were, I had something anchoring me through it all, the luminous white light that has lived inside me ever since I was a young girl.

As I got older, I felt a responsibility to this gift. I knew I should not and could not waste it. I wanted to go deep into studying the great spiritual teachers. I explored teachings from Judaism to Christianity to Buddhism. I learned yoga and studied with great yoga masters. I relished the words of mystic poets including Rumi and Hafiz. I learned how to meditate. I reignited my capacity for prayer. I learned the value of silence.

I also discovered profound wisdom—teachings from writers, scientists, and regular everyday folk from all backgrounds and ages. Inspiration and miracles are everywhere if you have the eyes to see them. I followed this quest over many years. I made it a priority to incorporate and live from the teachings I studied in every aspect of my life. As a result, my horizons expanded, and my life became richer.

It was a quiet and steady integration of teachings and spiritual wisdom for me over five decades. After my diagnosis of metastatic cancer in 2014, I began collecting quotes and poems that uplifted me. During that time, I began literally writing through my cancer. This book contains some of my favorite quotes, poems, and my personal writings since that time.

A wonderful surprise in writing this book was that I found how the themes interrelate and support each other. It was sometimes hard to choose which quote, poem, or writing fit best in which chapter. I hope you find this supports the idea that everything is connected.

You will notice in this book that, except for the introduction of the theme of each chapter, my personal writings are based on writing topics. Some people refer to them as prompts. In this book, I call them writing topics. Topics can be a word, phrase, or question. When a poem or quote is included in the topic, I refer to those as a poem prompt or a quote prompt.

I learned about this topic writing method when I participated in a Writing Through Cancer group at the University of California Medical Center where I was receiving my cancer care and treatment. When using this method, the writer is asked to write in response to the prompt or topic for 10–15 minutes without stopping. Throw grammar, editing, and anything else you learned about how to write out the window. Afterward, if writing in a group setting, as time allows and participants are willing, the writing is shared aloud without critique and without anyone commenting. What a huge relief. This method has given me the freedom to write whatever wanted to come through me without the fear or clamoring voice of the inner critic.

While participating in these writing groups, I was astounded at what I wrote and blown away at what others wrote in such short time segments using writing topics and poem and quote prompts. In this book, I have included some of my writings, with minimal editing. From 2016 until recently, I participated in six cohorts of Writing Through Cancer. The cancer writing groups were powerful and heart-wrenching. There were many times I looked forward to seeing my fellow writing friends only to find out that they had taken their last breath. It got very real, very quickly.

During this same time period, I took several in-person and online writing workshops with Natalie Goldberg, who is famous for the topic method of writing. Natalie is the author of fifteen books, most notably her seminal work, *Writing Down the Bones*. This book has sold over one million copies and has been translated into twelve languages. *Writing Down the Bones* was recently republished for its thirtieth anniversary.

Through the writing method laid out in her book, Natalie forever transformed the way writing is approached. If you trust it, it takes you deep, deep into your heart and mind. I consider Natalie one of my greatest teachers. The writing topic practice has been a godsend for me. It has been healing, heart opening, and fun. It has been a great comfort and friend through some very tough times.

During some of my most difficult stretches with cancer since 2019, I began and completed a two-year mindfulness meditation teacher training program with Jack Kornfield and Tara Brach, two world renowned meditation teachers. I was wholly committed to this study and I sometimes had to take my live classes on Zoom from the chemotherapy chair.

I finished my first required teacher training practicum in June of 2020 and my second teaching practicum between three hospitalizations in the fall of 2020, when I almost died from infections. I passed two comprehensive exams when I barely had energy to walk up the stairs. I share this not to congratulate myself, but as an acknowledgment of my dedication and how profoundly important mindfulness and meditation has been in my life.

I learned that even though I might be living with a life-threatening illness, it does not have to be front and center in my life. It does not have to consume me, although it has at times. I also learned that I can have many moments of joy and days of thriving while I am surviving and dying. I do not want to miss a moment of my life.

In this spirit, I took a chance on enrolling in my first Haiku writing workshop in February 2021. I had the great fortune to take the workshop with some masters of Haiku and Haiku history. The workshop was via Zoom and the instructors included Clark Strand, Kaz Tanahashi, Natalie Goldberg, and Roshi Joan Halifax.

Roshi Joan is an ordained Zen priest and the abbot and founder of the Upaya Zen Center in Santa Fe, New Mexico. The workshop, held yearly at Upaya for the past seven years, started with twenty-five participants. It had topped out around fifty people. In my February 2021 workshop, there were over 1,500 people attending from seventy-five countries.

Why would so many people want to attend a Haiku workshop? My guess is that Zoom makes workshops easier to attend and more affordable, and that our COVID-19 restrictions have given people more reasons to try things they might not otherwise attempt. That included me.

What is a Haiku? Haiku is a form of Japanese poetry dating back to the 1600s. A Haiku is, simply put, a poem in three lines and ideally seventeen syllables. The traditional Haiku follows a 5-7-5 pattern: the first line is five syllables, the second line is seven syllables, and the third line is five syllables.

Getting to the essence of something in three short lines is the challenge of writing a good Haiku. You know a great Haiku when your response to reading it is an "aha" moment. Haiku encapsulate a practice of mindfulness. Haiku traditionally include a reference to a season of the year, but they are not restricted to this. Haiku celebrate the moment and take exquisite notice of exactly what is happening in the moment. They have been the perfect poetic writing bridge to all I have learned about mindfulness and living in the moment.

As a student of Natalie's, I knew that I should just go for it and I have enjoyed the practice and challenge of writing Haiku. Even though I am a novice, I included some of my own Haiku poetry as a different type of my personal writing in the chapters of this book. I hope you enjoy them. If nothing else, they are short so they won't take too much of your time.

It is my hope that this little book opens you to a path of awakening or assists you on your path if you already have one. At minimum, I hope it supports you through dark days and uplifts you to see life from another perspective when you need it. I do not have all the answers and there is no one right path. What I do know is that having an awakening to something Greater, what I call the Divine, was and is the most sacred gift of my life, and I want to share it with you.

Chapter 1

GENEROSITY

"What if our Golden Rule were not only, "Do unto others as you would have them do unto you," but also "Give more to the world than you take from it"? That would change everything."

—Jacqueline Novogratz, *Manifesto for a Moral Revolution*

I am continually amazed when I hear a story about people who have so little or have reason to be bitter or closed-hearted, and how they respond to the needs of others with what seems like unbounded, unconditional generosity.

I find children and young people who do this to be especially inspiring. As the story goes, they hear about a need. They are moved to help. They find a way to get donations and raise money, sometimes in the six figures. One child, one person, inspired to help with a generous heart, starts the chain. What sparks this generous heart to take action?

A story I heard some years ago was about a ten-year-old girl, Aubyn Burnside, who was inspired to help kids being removed from their homes to go to a children's center to wait for foster care. Her older sister was a social worker and was sharing one night at the dinner table that the children she helped move out of their homes often only had a garbage bag to put a few of their clothes and things in when they were being taken from their home. The average child in foster care moves three to four times and traditionally carries his/her personal belongings from home to home in black garbage bags.

Aubyn immediately thought this was not right. She felt shame that what little these kids had was only worthy of putting into a garbage bag. She exclaimed to her parents and sister that she knew they had extra suitcases in their attic that were never used. She insisted her sister take some of that luggage so the foster kids would have a proper bag to put their things in. But she knew these few suitcases were not enough to meet the need. From there she went around her neighborhood asking for donations of suitcases people did not need or use.

This was in 1995, before social media or the widespread use of email, but word got out and Aubyn began to get so many donations, she had to get a warehouse to store all of the suitcases and bags. After that, with the help of others, Aubyn founded Suitcases for Kids, a not-for-profit organization in her home state of North Carolina, in an effort to provide all 300 Catawba County foster children with suitcases.

Aubyn's main goal became to train people to automatically donate their unused suitcases, backpacks, and duffels to children in foster care. The idea grew, just like recycling glass and newspaper, and brought in 4,000 suitcases from her local area in 1996. By the end of its first full year, Suitcases for Kids was in operation in nineteen states.

Aubyn developed a Starter Kit program for people and organizations that wanted to develop this program in their own community. In two years, the Suitcases for Kids organization grew into a national model and was active in all fifty states. Aubyn had personally collected over 17,000 suitcases.

Suitcases for Kids is now an international organization. The heart of this young girl, inspired by compassion and generosity, was able to make the lives of thousands of kids going into foster care a little better, a little more dignified.

I learned early on from my parents, Aggie and Hal, about service, giving back, and generosity. There was never a time when I was growing up that my parents were not volunteering their time, serving on a board of trustees of some not-for-profit organization, or raising or donating money. Their variety of service was astounding. It ranged from helping the poorest of the poor to raising money for college scholarships.

In 1994, my parents formed a small group to renovate an old building into a beautiful performing arts theater at the historic Chautauqua Institution in New York. They started their group, Friends of Chautauqua Theater, with five people and charged $10 dues to become a Friend of the Theater. My mom never wanted to leave anyone out due to their inability to pay. In three years, they raised millions of dollars to initiate and complete the renovation. The group still exists today, and the yearly dues are $25.

My dad taught me that no matter how much or how little you have, there are always ways to give. He also lived the principle of tithing, traditionally defined as giving back 10 percent of your income to a charity, church, or cause. He dutifully and happily did this and more every year to support many different organizations.

There are many creative ways to spread generosity. In 1999, for their fiftieth wedding anniversary, my parents decided they did not want a party or gifts and instead they sent fifty friends and family members $50. The only requirement was to donate this $50 to a worthy cause, organization, or individual and to write my folks a letter back with what they had done with the money and why.

Letters started pouring in. Many individuals decided to double the amount my parents had given them or even increase it tenfold. The letters were heartwarming and included personal stories of where the gifts were sent and why. The spirit of generosity opened people up. Secrets were revealed and burdens were lifted. In one letter my parents learned that longtime friends had a developmentally disabled grandchild. My mom kept the letters in a beautiful hand-painted box and they read them every year on their anniversary until she passed.

For my sixtieth birthday in 2018, I decided to shamelessly steal their idea. Connie and I sent $60 dollars to sixty friends and family asking the same thing. We also had a party and were able to share all the organizations and causes our loved ones' donations went to. As you might imagine, many of the conversations were about these organizations. We invite any and all of you to steal this idea as well if and when the time is right for you. I can guarantee the gifts you get back are more valuable than any present you will ever receive.

What I learned from my parents was that being generous and giving back is not an extra thing; it is something you do and how you live your life. I can truly say both my parents had generous hearts and they put this generous spirit into action in the world.

I have tried to emulate my parents' example in my life. Until my cancer came back, I volunteered at various organizations over the years. Giving is something Connie and I do every year. Some years we can do more than others, but we have always found a way to practice generosity, to be of service, and to give back through our time and resources.

~ QUOTES ~

The purpose of life is to discover your gift. The work of life is to develop it. The meaning of life is to give your gift away.
—*David Viscott*

It is not a question of whether you "have what it takes," but of whether you take the gifts you have . . . and share them with . . . the world.
—*Neale Donald Walsch*

Someone is sitting in the shade today because someone planted a tree a long time ago.
—*Warren Buffett*

Let us live a giving life. It is my awareness of what accompanies the giving act (the recognition of my reservations about giving, my resentment, my anxiety . . .) that slowly transforms me. It is the experience of my unkindness that can enable me to be truly kind.
—*Charlotte Joko Beck*

The cultivation of generosity is the beginning of spiritual awakening.
—*Sharon Salzberg*

One's philosophy is not best expressed in words; it is expressed in the choices one makes. . . . In the long run, we shape our lives and we shape ourselves. The process never ends until we die. And, the choices we make are ultimately our responsibility.

—Eleanor Roosevelt

~ POEM ~

"Golden Day"
by Danna Faulds

It is a golden day, a day
beholden to nothing but its
own sweet unfolding.
The only question is how
much of its richness can I
let in? How slowly can I walk
the leaf-strewn trail, inhaling
the goodness of the woods?
Just how blessed can I let myself be
in the midst of the world's chaos
and the unfailing generosity of trees?

PERSONAL WRITINGS

Writing Topic:
Write about Friends

Poem Prompt

"To a Friend Separated from Me by Illness,"
by Gretchen Fletcher

Our lives until so recently
parallel and filled
with common details
once thought boring,
now precious
paying phone bills
watering ferns
picking up car pools
dropping off dry cleaning—
details still in my life
while you lie in an alien bed
your life now filled with details
I don't know, tubes and shunts
and treatments tried and failed.
I want to speak; you want to speak,
but we've lost our common language.
You've learned a new vocabulary
I don't know. How can I know
how it feels to lose a breast
and fight to save lungs,

bone and brain
when all I have to battle
is the traffic?

My heart is filled with gratitude that my friends have been rock-solid supports for me through cancer. It has taught me a lot about friendship. Two friends in particular, Terri LeBeau and Mary Ann Papageorge, showed up for every chemotherapy session right after I was diagnosed with metastatic cancer, since Connie could not get away from her work. This particular chemotherapy in 2014 required eighteen infusions, once a week. Terri and Mary Ann showed up every week with sandwiches and my favorite potato chips. We munched and laughed the time away while my infusion pump dripped.

Terri and Mary Ann have been a constant and consistent thread of support, love, and laughter over many years and dark days as I navigate this cancer "journey" as it is often referred to. Their generosity of spirit and time has never wavered. I ask myself, could I be this generous to a friend?

Other friends checked in with email, calls, and texts. They helped me process what I feared was my death sentence. They listened and listened again. They made me laugh. They accepted it all—my hairless head, my puffy face, and my pale skin with funny spots.

Friends also gave me things like hats and blankets. They knew they could not take away my stage 4 diagnosis, but they wanted to do whatever they could for me. The things they gave me were not important; it was the symbol of their loving-kindness and the generosity of their hearts and their time. I think to give love, receive love, and know love are the greatest gifts of this human life. My friends have demonstrated that again and again.

My mind turns to my college friends Chris and Bruce. Tears run down my face as I write this. Chris and Bruce, "the wild and crazy guys" was what we nicknamed them my freshman year. That was 1977. Chris always called me Nanno. Chris's ears stuck out a bit and his big grin went from ear to ear. He was joyous and mischievous in the best way possible.

Chris was adored by my friend Barb and me. Even to this day, Chris's body now racked by head and neck cancer, barely able to speak and eat, the Chris we knew is still here, his spirit stronger than ever. Through it all, Chris in Ohio, Barb in New York, and me in California, we have remained friends.

Then there was Bruce, tall, smart, and handsome. Bruce, how did that microscopic bug get into you before our senior year? Was it encephalopathy or meningitis? I can't remember. But I remember hearing you succumbed, not to death, but that might have been a better option. No, this bug went to your brain and forevermore you would be four years old.

Chris was Bruce's best friend, and he is one of my heroes in the friendship department. He went to visit Bruce every year since 1981, until Bruce passed in 2014, for over thirty-three years. Bruce lived in Jamestown, New York, not a short drive from Cincinnati where Chris lived.

Bruce resided in a special home for people with brain injuries and disabilities. Feeling the profound, sad loss of the Bruce we knew, Chris never left him. Did Bruce remember Chris, the friend from college, or the new Chris who came to visit him? It did not matter to Chris. Bruce was his beloved friend. I know there were so many reasons Chris could have been doing something else, yet he faithfully went time and again and again to visit Bruce and his parents.

To me, Chris exemplified that when you are a true friend, the most important thing you can do is show up and give your friend your full attention. You don't make excuses, you give what you can of yourself, your time, your love, and your presence. It is one of the highest examples of a generous heart.

If there is a heaven, I know that Bruce is waiting to see Chris and welcome him. Bruce is waiting to resume where the two of them left off at age twenty-one, to finish the story. Oh please, let there be a Groundhog Day so Bruce and Chris can be together again.

Chris, you are the finest example of the most generous friend I have ever known. I can only hope you have a friend as good and true as you.

At the time of this original writing, Chris was still alive. Chris passed in 2019 of head and neck cancer. Bruce passed in 2014. *9/29/16*

Writing Topic:
Write about the Cancer Center

Quote Prompt

True heroism is remarkably sober, very undramatic. It is not the urge to surpass all others at whatever cost, but the urge to serve others, whatever the cost.

—Arthur Ashe

The cancer center has become a safe space. At first, it was alien and I certainly did not belong there. It was somewhere I went on a journey that had no map, or at least not a reliable one. A journey I did not want to be on.

It became somewhere to be held by a blue faux leather recliner where strange medicine was dripped into my body. Was there a floor below my feet? Some days it feels as if both the rug and the floor have been ripped out beneath me. I look around. So many others I do not know are on this same journey.

There are eighty chemotherapy drips going at the same time in the same room, each of us is separated by curtains. I hear moans, laughs, vomiting, whispered tones, frantic conversations all mixing together in a cancer center infusion stew.

The cancer center has become somewhere I go that I believe buys me more time on this earth with my precious Connie, all the while watching the minute hand move too fast, feeling I am in a race against the cancer cells gnawing on my bones and liver.

In the cancer center cocoon, I witness humanity, the best of it, in all its colors, shapes, and sizes. Beyond what is scary, pokey, sterile, rancid-smelling, dinging, painful, worrisome, uncertain, and fist-clenching dread, I witness generosity of spirit, one glance, one interaction at a time. It is a compassionate dance, all of us giving and receiving. I get a glimpse of how beautiful it all is. Perhaps, witnessing this, I don't need to ask for anything more. *3/20/17*

Haiku 2021

Lemonade

branches bowing down
lemons heavy with juice and pulp
they offer their life

Bouquet

spring erupts in color
the earth gives herself to us
yellow daffodils

Sacrifice

hot oil sizzles
waiting on the countertop
plump purple eggplant

QUESTIONS TO CONTEMPLATE

❀ When have you been moved to be generous?

❀ Is there a particular cause or organization's work that inspires you to practice generosity? If you are not already giving to them in some way, examine this more deeply and see how you might be of support.

❀ Generosity does not just mean giving of your time or resources to a big cause. It can be generosity of the heart through your kind words and deeds in the moment. It could mean giving more of your time, love, and compassion to a certain person. Who can you begin practicing generosity toward? ··

Chapter 2

CONNECTION

> "What will happen to us today is completely unknown. . . .
> Whatever happens, our commitment is to use it to awaken our
> heart. . . . All activities should be done with one intention.
> That intention is to realize our connection with all beings."
>
> —Pema Chödrön, The Places That Scare You

The word "connection" can mean so many things. It can be as simple as unplugging and plugging back in the connection of a computer or TV to reboot the device. Have we not all learned this the past fifteen-plus years, that before we pull our hair out and call someone to help, we must unplug and plug it back in first??

What I mean by connection in this book is the connection we feel with others, our communities, and the earth. It is often easy to recognize and feel connected with loved ones. Have you ever been thinking about a family member or friend and in the next five minutes they call or text you? Coincidence? Maybe.

Quantum physics tells us we are all linked at a vibrational level. Our thoughts are vibrations and they can move at lightning-fast speeds. Everything in the universe is literally connected. Many spiritual traditions refer to this concept as we are all One.

Nisargadatta Maharaj, a Hindu yogi who taught nondualism and whose collection of essays *I Am That* was published in 1973, summed up this sentiment of all being One when he said:

> *When you know beyond all doubting that the same life*
> *flows through all that is, and you are that life, then you*
> *will love all naturally and spontaneously.*

We have learned that babies in orphanages who are not regularly held and given an opportunity to feel a human connection can struggle as adults to trust, to love, and to feel loved. It seems to be vital from the time we are born to feel connection with other human beings.

Connection can also mean seeing ourselves in others. You feel the same way I do? What a relief. I recognize me in you and you in me and therefore, I am not alone. I have made a connection.

During my years living with cancer, I have been fortunate to be part of several support groups and Facebook groups for people living with cancer. I realized how much I needed this connection when I first searched for a support group in San Diego after my metastatic diagnosis. The groups were few and far between. I called some of the cancer centers and, to my amazement, they told me their groups were only for early-stage survivors. I cried. How could I be excluded?

Later I learned there was a Writing Through Cancer program at my medical center (University of California San Diego, or UCSD) facilitated by Sharon Bray Ed.D., who originally started a similar program at a cancer center in Northern California. I was thrilled! I immediately signed up only to learn soon after that the spring program had been postponed until the fall. I literally wept when I heard that news. While I had amazing support from family and friends, I desperately needed connection with others facing cancer. I would have to wait five more months.

The Writing Through Cancer groups helped me tremendously. I did not feel so alone on this journey when I could connect with other cancer patients. I learned that others also thought and felt many of the same things I did. I felt relief when others shared that they had the same strange side effects that the doctors never talk about. The group interaction was supportive and nonjudgmental, with no critique or commentary after someone read their writing. There was no need for it. I felt a deep, unspoken, loving connection with my fellow group members.

If we do not have or lose connection with others, our community, our nation, and our world, then we lose being in touch with the fabric of life. Our world's history is full of "othering." This group or that group is demonized and "othered" because of where they are from, the color of their skin, their sexual orientation, the language they speak, their political and religious beliefs. "Othering" is an easy out. Seeing each other's humanity beyond differences takes more work, takes a more evolved person.

This connection with community has been illustrated beautifully by the work of Father Gregory Boyle in Los Angeles. Father Boyle, or Father Greg as he is known, started working with gangs in Los Angeles in the 1980s. He wrote a magnificent book called *Tattoos on the Heart* documenting his journey and what he has learned. I was moved and inspired by this story and by the work of Father Greg.

Father Greg's initial assignment in 1985 was to be a priest for the Dolores Mission Church in one of the poorest neighborhoods of Los Angeles, Boyle Heights. The church was located between two housing projects and among the territories of numerous gangs.

Father Greg shares a story in his book that one morning when he was going to do a mass, he saw painted across the front of the church the words "wetback church." He was taken aback by the anti-immigrant fervor that we still know today and so he went to the sanctuary and gathered the folks who were there. He first apologized saying, "I feel so bad that we've been attacked in this way, that our sacred place has been desecrated. One of the things our kids do when they're coming out of the gangs is remove the tags and graffiti. It's one of their jobs. The city pays them to do this. So, I'll get them over here and get it off right away. I'm so, so sorry."

As he was saying that, one woman, Rosa Saldana, stood up. She was a little woman who never spoke. She shook her head and said, "You will not remove that." Father Greg said, "Please?" And then she went on. Rosa said, "If there are people who are cast out, judged, despised, rejected because they are *mojados*—wetbacks— then we shall be proud to call ourselves the wetback church."

Rosa was standing up for her community that she was connected to. Instead of wiping out the words, she invited everyone to embrace the connection and stand up for those called "wetbacks."

In Father Greg's work with the most violent of gang members, he found young people did not join gangs to belong to something; rather, they were fleeing something, most often violence, drugs, trauma, and shame. His program is based on creating a safe space, a "tender place of community" he calls it, where gang members are treated with respect. The focus of his program is on transformation, self-worth, and practical training and tools, not information and content to be imparted to those who do not know the difference between right and wrong.

In the 1990s Father Greg created Homeboy Industries. Today, Homeboy Industries is the largest and most successful gang rehabilitation and reentry program in the world. Homeboy Industries offers free services and programs, supporting around 10,000 men and women a year as they work to address their pasts, reimagine their futures, and emerge after eighteen months with jobs skills, self-worth, and hope for their future.

In an interview with the Bush Center, Father Greg shared, "Mother Teresa always talked about the problem in the world was that we'd forgotten that we belong to each other. We are inching closer to kinship, connection, and mutuality. We belong together. There's nobody outside the circle of compassion. The more you can assert that, the more people start to embrace."

In the summer of 2019, Connie and I made our annual visit to Chautauqua Institution (CHQ) in western New York State. Every summer, CHQ offers nine weeks packed with lectures, the arts, interfaith discussions, sports, and a wide variety of classes. That summer, some of the graduates of Homeboy Industries had been invited to speak. What a privilege it was to hear them share their stories and witness them telling about their personal transformation. Being of Latino and African American descent, proudly wearing tattoos and baggy pants, they stood out among the mostly white, educated, genteel Chautauquans and well-kept Victorian cottages and gardens. They were welcomed with open arms. So far from the barrios of Los Angeles, they made loving connections in small-town western New York.

The importance of connection for each of us individually and collectively cannot be underestimated. In fact, it may be the very thing that saves our planet. As we witness the growing effects of climate change, more and more people are waking up to the connection we have with our earth. We realize when we harm Mother Earth, we harm ourselves, our children, our grandchildren, greatgrandchildren, and many more generations to come.

In the course of history, there comes a time when humanity is called to shift to a new level of consciousness, to reach a higher moral ground. A time when we have to shed our fear and give hope to each other. That time is now.

—Wangari Maathai, Nobel Prize Laureate for the
Greenbelt Movement

I chose to include the theme of connection and the idea that we are all One in this book because it is so very vital to all of us personally and collectively. The more we understand it and embrace it, the better choices we will make and the more hope there is for our future.

~ QUOTES ~

Be brave enough to start a conversation that matters. . . . Expect to be surprised. Treasure curiosity more than certainty. . . .

Real listening always brings people closer.

Trust that meaningful conversations can change your world.
        —Margaret Wheatley, Turning to One Another

All is like an ocean, all flows and connects; touch it in one place and it echoes at the other end of the world.
                —Fyodor Dostoevsky

If everything is connected to everything else, then everyone is ultimately responsible for everything. . . . We find ourselves within a luminous organism of sacred responsibility.
        —Lawrence Kushner, Invisible Lines of Connection

*Be the most ethical, the most responsible, the most authentic
you can be with every breath you take, because you are cut-
ting a path into tomorrow that others will follow.*
—*Ken Wilber*

*We must remind ourselves that, although our lives are small
and our acts seem insignificant, we are generative elements
of the universe, and we create meaning with each act that we
perform or fail to perform.*
—*Kent Nerburn, Make Me an Instrument of Your Peace*

*Do your little bits of good where you are. It's those bits of
good put together that overwhelm the world.*
—*Desmond Tutu*

*How wonderful it is that nobody need wait a single moment
before starting to improve the world.*
—*Anne Frank*

*Each of us carries a unique spark of the divine, and each of
us is also an inseparable part of the web of life.*
—*Viktor Frankl*

~ POEMS ~

"Embers"
by Richard Wagamese

I don't want to touch you skin to skin.

I want to touch you deeply, beneath the surface, where our
real stories lie.

Touch you where the fragments of our being are, where the sediment of things that shaped us forms the verdant delta of our human story.

I want to bump against you and feel the rush of contact and ask important questions and offer compelling answers, so that together we might learn to live beneath the surface, where the current bears us forward deeper into the great ocean of shared experience.

This is how I want to touch and be touched—through beingness—so that someday I might discover that even skin remembers.

"Caretake This Moment"
by Epictetus

Caretake this moment.
Immerse yourself in its particulars.
Respond to *this* person, *this* challenge, *this* deed.

Quit the evasions.
Stop giving yourself needless trouble.
It is time to really live; to fully inhabit the situation you happen to be in now.
You are not some disinterested bystander.
Exert yourself.

Respect your partnership with providence.
Ask yourself often, how may I perform this particular deed
such that it would be consistent with and acceptable to the
     divine will?
Heed the answer and get to work.

When your doors are shut and your room is dark you
     are not alone.

The will of nature is within you as your natural genius
    is within.
Listen to its importunings.
Follow its directives.

As concerns the art of living, the material is your own life.
No great thing is created suddenly.
There must be time.

Give your best and always be kind.

PERSONAL WRITINGS

Writing Topic:
Making Connection

Quote Prompt

The hungers that live in the human heart are part of the kinship
that threads all of us together. We are interdependent beings with
a profound need both to give and to receive from one another.
What one of us is lacking, another has in abundance, whether that
be a bowl of rice, a skill, a wisdom, a capacity for joy, a knowledge,
or a courageous heart. Our urges and our gifts, our longings and
our offerings, are all needed and all indispensable.
    —John Robbins and Ann Mortifee, *The Awakened Heart*

Poem Prompt

"Dreaming the Dark"
by Starhawk

Community.
Somewhere, there are people
to whom we can speak with passion
without having the words catch in our throats.
Somewhere a circle of hands will open to receive us,
eyes will light up as we enter, voices will celebrate with us
whenever we come into our own power.
Community means strength that joins our strength
to do the work that needs to be done.
Arms to hold us when we falter.
A circle of healing. A circle of friends.
Someplace where
we can be free.

I have heard it said that if you have one true friend in your lifetime, that is enough. I have been blessed to have a number of people in my life who have fit this "true friend" for me. One of them is my lifelong friend Cammy Oster, whom I met when I was three years old. We had just moved to a new house in a community called Rocky River. And, yes, there was a Rocky River in the town that fed into Lake Erie.

Cammy and I lived five houses apart. Cammy's family home was on the corner of our street, Westhaven Lane, in the farm house her Finnish grandfather built. Cammy came from a large Catholic family, with four older brothers, two younger brothers, and one younger sister. I came from a solidly Protestant family, with one older sister.

We were the same age and went from kindergarten through our senior year in high school at the same schools. I think we were soul-mate friends since the day we met. Through the years, especially in the later grade school years, people often mixed us up, thinking we were twins or at least sisters. Our physical resemblance was uncanny.

Growing up, I could not spend enough time at Cammy's house. We had a special connection. The house was warm and welcoming. Her Mom always had something wonderful-smelling on the stove or in the oven. The wild and unpredictable nature of each day with eight children was something I relished.

During our grade school years, I would make my way to Cammy's house shortly before 8 am. With our other friends, we would walk the mile to school along Wooster Road, back and forth for lunch, and then home again after school. We, as well as our parents, thought nothing about us walking four miles a day. The weather had to be exceptionally dangerous or cold for us not to make the trek. We begged to ride our bikes when we were old enough even if there was still ice on the sidewalks. We loved being outside.

As we worked our way up to puberty, Cammy's older brothers made it their mission to bug and torment us. They would pick their nose and throw boogers at us. They would fart into their hands and cover our faces with the nasty smell. We made it our mission to stay out of their sight.

Cammy's front yard had two huge buckeye trees. If you don't know about buckeye trees, they grow large and strong and produce nuts in the fall. The nuts are covered in a chartreuse green shell with spikes poking out. They crack open when they fall or when ten-year-old hands pry them open. These are not nuts you can eat, but we loved collecting brown paper bags full of them anyway and smelling their earthy smell.

One of the two buckeye trees in Cammy's front yard was perfect for climbing. We spent a good amount of time every day over the summers after fifth and sixth grades living in that tree. When our tree fortress was attacked by booger-throwing brothers, we would round the yard and sneak up into the garage rafters, our special secret hiding place.

Two large sheets of plywood balanced across the garage rafters made a nice platform that we covered with old blankets and pillows. We would climb up an old wooden ladder spattered with layers of paint and then rest it along the wall close enough so we could reach it, but far enough away it would not lend suspicion that the two of us were up there. We talked for hours on end in the buckeye tree and in the rafters with a limitless number of topics to cover. Our friendship bond and connection deepened.

One summer evening in junior high, two other friends came over to camp with us in Cammy's backyard tent. We stayed up most of the night. We raided the neighbor's strawberry patch after midnight. We added these strawberries to Cammy's Mom's already-made giant bowl of strawberry compote, and ate strawberry shortcake and drank homemade lemonade until our stomachs hurt and there were sticky puddles of red all over the kitchen counters and floor.

That night in the tent, we talked about boys and boys some more. We compared our breast sizes. We showed each other our bras, examining them like finely woven linen. I had no idea what gay was then nor did it cross my mind. We were completely focused on what connected us and that was moving from girlhood to puberty, gently letting go of our childhood and anxiously awaiting young adulthood.

What may have really solidified our lifetime connection was one winter day in junior high. Overnight, there had been a bad winter storm. As was the custom, all the parents would watch the morning news to see if the schools in our district had closed. A little ticker tape went by at the bottom of the TV screen listing the schools as open or closed. To our astonishment that day, our junior high was listed as open. I called Cammy. I walked to her house in my black boots, heavy coat, and wool scarf, hat, and mittens.

We set off on the two-mile walk to school and could barely see a foot in front of us. The wind howled and snow was falling. The sidewalks were not shoveled. We saw no cars or people, yet we continued on, occasionally looking at each other but not saying a word. When we reached a huge shopping center parking lot we used as a short cut, there was nothing to block the wind. It howled and what little of our faces was exposed was covered in wet snow. We bent forward to move onward in the face of what I guess may have been fifty-mile-per-hour gusts. Still, I was with my best friend. We were not going to give up. We could do this.

Navigating around and over piles of snow left by earlier snow plowing, we saw something in the distance coming toward us. It looked like a shadowy mirage. As it got closer, we realized it was a fellow student from junior high. When we crossed his path in the parking lot, the only words he uttered were that the junior high was closed. With bright-red cheeks poking out of our scarves, we looked at each other and turned around, grateful now the wind was at our backs.

We got home safely with frozen toes and wet jackets. When I came in the door, I loudly announced the junior high was closed, no school. My mom casually looked up from her magazine and said, "I know."

There are so many stories I could share about my connection and friendship with Cammy, now known as Cameron Plagens. She has degrees in art and art therapy and a PhD in psychology. She raised three amazing daughters. After I finished college and moved to California, we drifted apart only to reconnect in our thirties, picking up just where we left off, not missing a beat.

Cammy's friendship has meant the world to me. We are truly soul sisters. We laugh and cry together. We are radically honest with each other. We support each other. I dare say she listens to me more than I do her. She has been an invaluable, wise ear as I have navigated the ups and downs of living with cancer. She still lives in the area near where we grew up, but has a mostly different circle of friends now. Yet, I managed to convince her to go to our fortieth high school reunion. She was skeptical, but we thoroughly enjoyed ourselves. Our connection as friends has been one of the most precious gifts of my life. There are not enough words to thank her for being my lifelong friend. 2021

Writing Topic:
The Truth about Me Is

Quote Prompt

We are all affecting the world every moment, whether we mean to or not. Our actions and states of mind matter, because we are so deeply interconnected with one another.

—Ram Dass

Poem Prompt

"Untitled" by
Judith Morley

By what miracle
Does the cracker
Made from Kansas wheat,
This cheese ripened in French caves,
This fig, grown and dried near Ephesus,
Turn into me?
My eyes,
My hands,
My cells, organs, juices, thoughts?

Am I not then the Kansas wheat
And French cheese
And Smyrna figs?
Figs, no doubt,
The ancient Prophets ate?

The truth about me is I am constantly learning, evaluating, growing, stalling, and growing again. Many times, I circle around the same familiar block before I "get it." I believe the adage "An unexamined life is not worth living." Note: I often do not get quotes exactly right. It may be due to my Sagittarius astrology sign, close enough is good enough most of the time.

I can be hard on myself as well as others despite my typically optimistic outlook on life. I have been known to go to the dark side in a nanosecond but generally pull myself out quickly. I don't dwell there. Perhaps that is genetics.

What I do know is that I have learned the most from those that push my buttons. Now that I know this, I have no excuse anymore. It is usually me looking in a mirror seeing something I do not want to own about myself. If you ever want to know more about your shadow side and how powerful this work is, look no further than Debbie Ford's *Dark Side of the Light Chasers* book. Sadly, Debbie passed of cancer, but her work lives on through her fifteen books and the Ford Institute she started.

What I have learned is that it is all me, that it is all, all of us, we all are everything, and everything is us. We are all connected. In yogic circles they call it "I AM THAT." Once you embrace this, it is easy sailing. Getting there and staying there is the tricky part. Taking up residence in a higher vibration is where I want to pay rent. In fact, it is the only place. *11/20/19*

Haiku 2021

Eternal Connectedness

death is an illusion
don't cry for me connie villa
i'll always love you

QUESTIONS TO CONTEMPLATE

❀ Where do you feel most deeply connected and why?

❀ Where do you feel disconnected and why?

❀ Do you believe everyone and everything in the universe is connected? If this were to be true, is it important? How does it relate to your life (or not)?

Chapter 3

COMPASSION

"*Compassion changes everything. Compassion heals. Compassion mends the broken and restores what has been lost. Compassion draws together those who have been estranged or never even dreamed they were connected. Compassion pulls us out of ourselves and into the heart of another, placing us on holy ground where we instinctively take off our shoes and walk in reverence.*"

—Judy Cannato, Field of Compassion

What is compassion? It is not sympathy or pity. It is not empathy. The truest meaning of compassion is to recognize the suffering of others and take action. Empathy is a step toward compassion. Empathy is understanding how someone feels and imagining how you might feel in the same situation. Compassion is a tangible expression of love for those who have significant unmet needs or are suffering. Compassion does not judge.

It is said we must be able to have compassion for ourselves if we are truly and freely able to give it to others. In *Buddha's Little Instruction Book,* Jack Kornfield shares, "If your compassion does not include yourself, it is incomplete."

Self-compassion may be the most difficult first step as we are often hardest on ourselves. When I fall into this pattern, I stop and notice what I am doing and consciously remind myself to have some self-compassion. Pema Chödrön, ordained Buddhist nun, author, and teacher, says it beautifully: "Compassion isn't some kind of self-improvement project or ideal that we are trying to live up to. Having compassion starts and ends with having compassion for all the unwanted parts of ourselves, all the imperfections that we don't even want to look at." Self-compassion was something I had to learn as an adult. It was eye-opening. It is still a work in progress.

There are many ways to practice compassionate action. Compassion can be found in very simple things. It might be praying for another person's welfare and highest good. It could be taking your elderly neighbor's trash out every week after you notice them struggling to do so. It could mean volunteering your time at a women's shelter or watching a neighbor's child after school until a parent gets home from work. Whether it is a large act or a small one, compassion is needed in our world. Never underestimate what a difference you might make in someone's life by practicing it. The Dalai Lama puts it this way, "Compassion and love are not mere luxuries, as the source of both inner and external peace, they are fundamental to the continual survival of our species."

A beautiful example of compassion in action is my sister, Janine Obee. For five years, Janine did volunteer work for Pages Opening People (POP), an organization in Asheville, North Carolina, where she lives. POP's mission is to give people greater access to reading by redistributing books to those who have limited means and access.

My sister learned about POP in 2013. It had two people running it and doing all the work. At that time, POP was only able to distribute books to adults and organizations serving adults. When Janine talked to the directors, she learned they had a warehouse full of thousands of children's books and no capacity to distribute them. This was a real shame because in the Asheville area, 61 percent of lower-income homes have zero age-appropriate books for their children.

It was a match made in heaven, as they say, because my sister's graduate degree was in childhood development. At age sixty she tackled this project with love and devotion. She cleaned, repaired, and sorted the books by age level. This was back-breaking work and took an enormous amount of time. In addition, Janine had to find organizations and schools that would accept and distribute the books.

What she did not know was how much red tape could be involved. Overcoming all of the obstacles, she connected with organizations including Head Start, the Western Carolina Rescue Mission, CARING for Children, and local churches and schools to get books to families in need. In four years, she single-handedly distributed over 10,000 lovingly restored books for kids from preschool through high school who might otherwise not have a book in their home.

This chapter's theme, Compassion, is dedicated to my sister. We learned the value of service and giving back from our parents. Janine has never lost sight of living this value. Many of us will be moved by hearing a story of need or suffering, but it takes a special person to roll up their sleeves and put this compassion into action. In the words of Meister Eckhart, "Those who follow compassion find life for themselves, justice for their neighbors and glory for God."

~ QUOTES ~

Compassion is the keen awareness of the interdependence of all things.

—*Thomas Merton in The Mystic Hours*
by Wayne Teasdale

Try to feel compassion for how difficult it is to be an imperfect human being in this extremely competitive society of ours. Our culture does not emphasize self-compassion, quite the opposite. We're told that no matter how hard we try, our best just isn't good enough.

—*Kristin Neff*

Action expresses priorities.

—*Mahatma Gandhi*

We can each be part of what the world is trying to become. And that is no small matter. . . . The stakes are high, the responsibility profound, and the heart of humanity is at stake.
—*Adyashanti, "Foreword" in The Deep Heart*
by John J. Prendergast

It's in that convergence of spiritual people becoming active and active people becoming spiritual that the hope of humanity now rests.

—*Van Jones*

~ POEMS ~

"Mimesis"
by Fady Joudah

my daughter wouldn't hurt a spider
That had nested
Between her bicycle handles
For two weeks
She waited until it left of its own accord

If you tear down the web I said, it will simply know
This isn't a place to call home
And you'd get to go biking

 She said that's how others
Become refugees isn't it?

"Compassion"
by Miller Williams

Have compassion for everyone you meet,
even if they don't want it.

What seems conceit,
bad manners, or cynicism is always a sign

of things no ears have heard, no eyes have seen.
You do not know what wars are going on
down there where the spirit meets the bone.

PERSONAL WRITINGS

Writing Topic:
Write a Letter to a Body Part

Letter to my heart. As far as I know you have always been a good, strong heart. You love, you have compassion, and you forgive. When I am sad and grieve, you ache. It is a deep ache. This ache has widened over the years like a huge rock crevice breaking open with no bottom in sight. But that crevice has opened me to people, places, things, and circumstances that I otherwise would not have known or have loved. It has taught me how to live with more compassion.

I thank you, heart, for your endurance, for continuing to keep me alive despite now having some consequences from years of medicine designed to rid my body of cancer; that has not necessarily been easy on you. So now my little heart pumps with a low "ejection fraction" they call it, and I need medication that I do not understand, but do understand will help regulate you.

Some cancer treatments have caused high blood pressure. At times, my blood pressure has been dangerously low. This can't be good on you. And now, there is a slight effusion around you according to my latest echocardiogram. Can you imagine? Fluid with cancer in it surrounds you, my heart? Oh, my heart, stay strong. I do not know what it all means, but I can guess that if the cancer does not get me first, some wear and tear on you will.

I have to ask myself, have I loved enough? Are there enough beats left for me to LOVE EVERYONE as the famous spiritual teacher Ram Dass tells us his teacher, Neem Karoli Baba, instructed him to do? Can I have enough compassion to take action when needed no matter how small or insignificant I think it might be?

It is ironic how a heart beats and a clock ticks (or at least they did before clocks were digital). Either way, it seems that is how you count time. Time is not the friend of those of us with advanced cancer, but you, my heart, can always be my friend, down to the last soft tick. Thank you for allowing me to feel love and compassion in greater quantities than I ever thought humanly possible. Thank you for all the beats you have given me, and those that I hear today and those that I hope are yet to come. *1/18/18*

Writing Topic:
An Animal I Love Is?

Is there a greater love on this planet than that of a dog? Well, yes, but many days it feels like it is the best love of all—unconditional, enthusiastic, loyal, and unbounded. All of this and more was Jake, the Westie we had for fifteen years. I miss that "little white dog," as our three-year-old neighbor, Zion, called him. Is he running somewhere in the green fields of heaven? Does he have doggie angel wings? I like to imagine that.

Will I ever see him again? I love the thought that I will. Did we do right by him? The hospice and palliative care veterinarian said, "You don't want to wait a day too late." Were we compassionate in our decision to "put him down"? It felt kind and cruel at the same time. How could we ever make that decision? Was this the truest form of compassion we could give him?

The thought of Jake in pain, suffering and frightened if we had to take him to a busy vet's office or an after-hours animal hospital was too much to bear. No, we did not want that. That would not be our goodbye.

Do "it" at home where Jake feels comfortable and safe. He knows the smells; they are familiar and friendly. I prayed Jake would show us a sign that it was indeed his time to say goodbye. That "little white dog" did show us a sign, an unmistakable one.

Those last couple of weeks Jake was alive, he was weak, could barely see or hear, but still managed to take himself outside to do his business via the long walk to the garage, through the doggie door, and down the side of the house to the little patch of green grass in our backyard. What spirit still does this that is barely able to walk?

One night at 2 am, Jake dragged his bone-thin body downstairs and outside where he tried to dig a hole in a corner of the yard filled with river rocks. We had heard that dogs go away from the "pack" when they are dying to keep their pack safe. They often dig a hole to die in. We heard Jake digging in the corner of the yard that night. Connie brought him inside and back upstairs to our bed. An hour later, he was doing the same thing. Jake gave us the sign, a gift of knowing it was the right time to say goodbye, which is what I had prayed for. If dogs could take compassionate action, this was it. Jake did that for us.

In those last days, we gave Jake whatever he wanted to eat, things supposedly not good for dogs, including small bits of hot dogs and bacon. He had refused to eat the special kidney dog food prescribed for him. His tail wagged one last time the day before we said goodbye when I gave him a small stuffed animal like I had dozens of times before. Our Jake was still there.

Being with him that last day before the vet came, watching him sleep in a corner of the family room he never slept in before, I wanted to suspend, no, I wanted to reverse, time. I could not say goodbye to this dog I loved with every fiber of my being. My heart broke open again and again.

The final day was grueling. Time passed slowly and too quickly. Then saying the final goodbye. Thanking him. There were not enough words to express the joy he gave us. Holding him, watching him take his last breath, the tears and sobs consumed my entire being. Walking with him while Connie carried him to the car that would take his little body away. How could we not be with him until the last second?

It was what I did for both of my parents just months before, giving them all the dignity and love I could in my goodbye. So they would not be alone, I walked beside the stretcher taking them from their room to the morgue transport that would take their bodies away forever. A deep sadness overcame me.

A beautiful green quilt covered my father. That summer morning, July 16, was fresh and dewy, bursting with life. A day my dad would have loved to be playing golf. My mother had a blue quilt over her. The night of October 20th was cold and rainy. There were still autumn leaves on the trees. My mom would have loved that.

Did they suffer? I do not know. Was it their time? I believe so. I want to believe that. It is just so damn hard to believe, no matter what your age or circumstance or how much you have loved or not loved yet, that it is your time to pass when you go. Who wrote that law? And so, how do we go on living? How do we live now without that "little white dog"? *11/2017*

Haiku 2021

Container

compassion like the sky
a vast place so huge it
can hold all the world's sorrow

Laughter Is the Best Medicine

awoke early one dawn
Buddha why are you laughing
he laughed and laughed more

QUESTIONS TO CONTEMPLATE

❧ Where have you seen compassion in action?

❧ What stories of compassion have touched you the most in your life?

❧ Have you ever received compassion?

❧ Did you ever recognize a time you could have been compassionate but were not? If so, why do you think that was?

❧ Do you think practicing acts of compassion has some value for your life, your loved ones, your neighbors, and our world?

Chapter 4

GRATITUDE

> "*If the only prayer we say in our lifetime is "thank you," that would suffice.*"
>
> —Meister Eckhart

I do not know when, but gratitude became a cornerstone of my daily life at some point in my adulthood. Gratitude has given me much-needed perspective on the ups and downs of life. We all have times of hardship, sorrow, loss, and illness, but when I zoom out enough, even in the most difficult of times, there was and is much to be grateful for. I never have to look any further than the evening news or now my iPhone newsfeed to gain this perspective. When I read or hear about what others are going through, I am beyond grateful for what I have and the love all around me.

Even in my darkest days of cancer—receiving bad news, suffering the harsh side effects of treatment, and being in the hospital—I never lost sight of gratitude. In fact, in the fall of 2020 when I was hospitalized three times in three months due to serious life-threatening infections, gratitude poured out of me from my hospital bed.

Everyone, starting with Connie, and everything I thought about became a spark for the practice of gratitude. I found myself weeping from my hospital bed out of this place of gratitude, not out of the fear or pain I was feeling, but a feeling of a deep bow of gratefulness for this life I have been given, the life I have lived. Everything from my life came into focus in the hospital. I began spontaneously praying to my deceased parents and thanking them for things I never thanked them for before. The thought of others to thank began to bubble up as well. I would thank them one by one.

I have always had profound gratitude for the medical care I have received over many years, and at this time in the hospital, even more so. The kind, compassionate, and competent care I received from the doctors, nurses, and staff in the middle of the COVID pandemic was extraordinary. I found tears running down my face during many of my encounters with these individuals helping me get to and from the bathroom, hanging bags of fluids and antibiotics, bringing me extra pillows and blankets for comfort. Those who brought my meal trays and those who cleaned my room touched me very deeply. Every day, taking care of me, they risked exposure to a virus that might kill them. My gratitude door opened wide.

Out of this profound gratitude, miracles started to happen. People I wanted or needed to talk to connected with me, including two pastors—one did not know I was in the hospital and one came on his rounds and happened to have extra time to spend with me. The miracles that happened are too numerous to mention, but they flowed continually. It was as if I had been given a new pair of eyes to see them. Gunilla Norris, author of *Simple Ways* and a series of books on what she calls "household spirituality," describes how I felt, "The world, our lives, our daily bread, our loved ones, our opportunities, our challenges and difficulties—all are gifts. . . . There is not a single moment in life in which we are not given something. . . . Showered with blessings, it will take our entire lifetime to learn to be nothing but a living thankfulness."

I was sad and scared that I might die never seeing Connie again. In fact, my first hospitalization was over Connie's birthday. I cried and cried until nothing was left. I just wanted to be home. The nurse taking care of me that day stopped to get a card, flowers, and a happy birthday sign for me to give to Connie. My doctors were on the fence as to whether to let me go home, but they did. I would have leapt into their arms to express my gratitude if I could have. The possibility of not being able to say goodbye to the people I love and not having a chance to finish this book was hard to face. It felt heavy, yet the gratitude I felt lifted my spirit and pointed me in a direction to fully trust in something greater than myself. I surrendered to this trust and lived from a place of complete gratitude.

~ QUOTES ~

It is through gratitude for the present moment that the spiritual dimension of life opens up.

—Eckhart Tolle

In ordinary life we hardly realize that we receive a great deal more than we give, and that it is only with gratitude that life becomes rich.

—Dietrich Bonhoeffer

The happy heart is one that is filled with gratitude. A simple ritual such as bowing and breathing deeply to greet each day awakens the joy in us. Each day, each season, each cycle offers something of beauty. Let us notice and give thanks.

—Diane Mariechild, Open Heart

Piglet noticed that even though he had a very small heart, it could hold a large amount of gratitude.

—A. A. Milne, Winnie the Pooh

Gratitude can transform ordinary common things into thanksgivings.

—William Arthur Ward

It is not joy that makes us grateful; it is gratitude that makes us joyful.

—Brother David Steindl-Rast

~ POEM ~

"The Lanyard"
by Billy Collins

The other day I was ricocheting slowly
off the blue walls of this room,
moving as if underwater from typewriter to piano,
from bookshelf to an envelope lying on the floor,
when I found myself in the L section of the dictionary
where my eyes fell upon the word *lanyard.*

No cookie nibbled by a French novelist
could send one into the past more suddenly—
a past where I sat at a workbench at a camp
by a deep Adirondack lake
learning how to braid long thin plastic strips
into a lanyard, a gift for my mother.

I had never seen anyone use a lanyard
or wear one, if that's what you did with them,
but that did not keep me from crossing
strand over strand again and again
until I had made a boxy
red and white lanyard for my mother.

She gave me life and milk from her breasts,
and I gave her a lanyard.
She nursed me in many a sick room,
lifted spoons of medicine to my lips,
laid cold face-cloths on my forehead,
and then led me out into the airy light

and taught me to walk and swim,
and I, in turn, presented her with a lanyard.
Here are thousands of meals, she said,
and here is clothing and a good education.
And here is your lanyard, I replied,
which I made with a little help from a counselor.

Here is a breathing body and a beating heart,
strong legs, bones and teeth,
and two clear eyes to read the world, she whispered,
and here, I said, is the lanyard I made at camp.
And here, I wish to say to her now,
is a smaller gift—not the worn truth

that you can never repay your mother,
but the rueful admission that when she took
the two-tone lanyard from my hand,
I was as sure as a boy could be
that this useless, worthless thing I wove
out of boredom would be enough to make us even.

PERSONAL WRITINGS

Writing Topic:
Make a List of What I Am Grateful For

This list could go on for days and weeks. Here is what jumps to my mind today in this ten-minute write:

Being born
Being loved
Being whole
Having a spiritual awakening
Potato chips
Chips and salsa
Jamocha almond fudge ice cream
Two legs, two arms, two feet
Ability to laugh and play
Ability to serve others
Forgiveness
Riding a bike, having a bike
Travel
Family and friends
Warm blankets
Avocados
Coffee with half and half
Our pups and kitties
Warm ocean water
Cool breezes
School
Teachers

Meditation and yoga
Fabulous medical care
Having time to slow down and enjoy the moments
Most of all—CONNIE

I am not sure how to express all the gratitude I have for Connie, my partner, my friend, my spouse. I feel it every day. I live it. I hope I express it in 1,001 ways so she knows it deep down in her bones.

Why am I so grateful for this relationship with my beloved? Everything on the list, everything in my life is enhanced through and with her love. Sharing life with her has made it so much sweeter. To "have and to hold" and to have someone to go through life with is something I do not take for granted.

It has been a blessing to have Connie with me through the ups and downs of life. I learn from her. We have a beautiful reciprocity in our relationship. We have trust, respect, honesty, and love. I have someone who knows me at my best and my worst, and still loves me. She has truly lived the wedding vow "in sickness and in health." Connie stands by my side every day as companion, lover, friend, partner, caregiver, and spouse. I feel like I won the lottery with her. I did.

Not everyone gets a long-term partner. Still, love abounds in so many ways. I trust I would have found it anyway, in a different way, and yet I know there are no sweeter words or thoughts than being with my Connie. *4/15/19*

Writing Topic:
Write about the Body

Quote Prompt

Let us keep ourselves open to the power that carries our life in every moment . . . that we may be filled with silent gratefulness.

—Paul Tillich

Today I want to be in praise and thanksgiving about my body—what it has withstood and despite all of it, I am still standing and breathing. Since 2005 over ten different cancer treatments, mostly chemotherapy, toxic chemicals designed to kill fast-growing cancer cells infused directly into my veins and targeted down to a microgram to destroy lesions I never met.

How many dozens of MRIs and CT scans have I endured? I have lost count. Well over 100. Learning to hold still and hold my breath. Trying to calm my mind and my heart for an hour when the loud clangs and bangs of the MRI stimulate the fight-flight response. And then the chemical "contrast" blasted into my veins to better light up the problem areas. Who knows how toxic that has been to my body?

And, I have taken hormone-suppressing prescriptions and shots over many years. One particularly memorable set of shots involved the drug Faslodex. Faslodex is given via one of those huge needles you really should not look at or see even from the corner of your eye. I had fifteen months of these shots given every three weeks.

During my first shot, a nurse new to giving the drug inserted the needle and the ice-cold just-out-of-the-refrigerator drug directly into the center of each of my butt cheeks. What neither of us knew was that the shot protocol was to not give it in the center of each buttock, but to be off to the side by a couple of inches, and have the Faslodex shot warmed to room temperature.

Each shot was to be given slowly over two minutes. She acted as though this was the Kentucky Derby. Both shots were given in under one minute. The next day, I woke up with huge black-and-blue marks spanning the width of my butt cheeks, one faintly resembling Indonesia and one resembling Malaysia. Try and sit on those!

And then there are all the side effects of different cancer treatments my body has tolerated. As Forrest Gump said, they are "like a box of chocolates, you never know what you are going to get," and in the case of chemotherapy, to what degree. Trying to stay calm and grounded when it feels like a civil war is raging inside my body is no small feat. So much ammunition, so many fronts to fight, so many things coming at my body all at once. I marvel in its resilience.

Today I am in praise and awe of this body. I want to ask it for more miles like a reliable old car you love and want to keep. I hope my engine runs for a long time. And, of course, that the brakes will continue to work when needed. Thank you, my dear body. How can I ever thank you enough, you have done way more than I ever thought I would ask of you. *4/18/19*

Writing Topic:
Write an Homage to a Body Part

Poem Prompt

"homage to my hips"
by Lucille Clifton

these hips are big hips
they need space to
move around in.
they don't fit into little
petty places. these hips
are free hips.
they don't like to be held back.
these hips have never been enslaved,
they go where they want to go
they do what they want to do.

Homage to My Feet

Sometimes I need to get off of this cancer topic even though this program is called Writing Through Cancer. Today I want to pay homage to my feet.

To begin with, my feet have always been a bit smaller than the average woman's foot at a 6½ shoe size. That, in itself, is not an issue, but my feet are wider than the average woman's feet. That is a problem.

Couple a wide foot with the fact that pointy-toed shoes with razor thin heels have been popular for most of my life and you have a real issue on your hands, or should I say feet? And then there was the challenge of my second and third toes being longer than my big toe (a sign of intelligence I was assured by my mother). There is never enough room at the end of a lady's pump for these toes.

Undaunted, I wore these pieces of leather hell for years. My toes squished, balls of my feet on fire until they went numb, still wearing a silly grin on my face, I pranced along in these shoes. I mastered the ability to ignore the sensation of a vise grip and nails jabbing into the sides of my feet as I clicked along at work doing whatever I was doing.

Would you like to wear torture chambers on your feet? Why, yes, I think I would. I will take this pair in black and in navy blue. I would like to move up to the more advanced class of wearing these torture chambers.

Who on God's green earth and in what man-made hell was the wearing of these devices ever invented and sold to millions of women? God only knows what damage a four-inch heel permanently does to your pelvic tilt. I think mine went in the wrong direction.

Despite the torturous hell I put my feet through, they kept going. I have kept going. I now wear what they call sensible shoes. I don't care if I look like a nun or an old lady—I aspire to be the latter. Give me sensible shoes any day as long as they take me on the sacred journey of life and allow me to have another day on this incredible earth. Better yet? Give me bare feet in the green grass, in the sand, in the mud, or in warm blue ocean water. Bring it on! *4/8/19*

Writing Topic:
Write about the Body #2

The first thing that occurs to me is that I am glad to still be in my body. I want more time in this body. Maybe one day I won't, but today, right now, I do. Like many women, I have had and continue to have many criticisms about my body—this is too big, that is too small, not enough of this, too much of that. I always wanted to have thick, curly hair. Well, now that I have lost my hair three times, I am just glad to have hair. Update: As of 2021, I have lost my hair five times in sixteen years.

How does one make peace with the body that, after all, let cancer sneak in? And then, after cancer was hopefully banished forever, my body let it sneak in again, this time with whistles, bells, and a band taking up permanent residence in my bones and liver.

Yet I want to make peace with this body. It has endured so many things—surgeries, chemotherapy, radiation, and all their side effects. And if indeed X-rays, CT scans, MRIs, and bone scans make you radioactive, then with the dozens I have had I could light up New York City.

And then there is the wear and tear on my heart, liver, and kidneys from all the different treatments. So far, I am able to keep on ticking, eliminating and ridding my body of toxins, but who knows how long the warranties on these body parts are?

I know others who have abused their bodies with drugs and alcohol and are doing fine well into their seventies and eighties. I have known others who are poster children for good health. They exercise, eat right, and some are vegans and vegetarians. Yet some of these healthy specimens have not escaped the clutches of cancer, heart attacks, strokes, and other diseases. Maybe it is genetics. Maybe it is all a big crap shoot. I don't know.

This life sometimes feels like a game of Pin the Tail on the Donkey: someone blindfolds you, spins you around, then gives you a paper donkey tail with a pin on the end, and you are supposed to walk forward and literally pin the tail on the ass of a donkey on a poster hanging on the wall. I remember as a child at my sixth birthday party we played this game. I totally missed the donkey's ass and pinned the tail on his nose.

Most of us will miss the mark. So we might as well go through life with all we have; leave nothing back and nothing out. Live and love loudly, deeply, fully, and completely. It does not matter if your tail is missing, crooked, or on your nose. It does not matter what body I was issued; I can still dance and sing until I can't anymore. I will cherish this body until my last breath and then offer it back to the wind, the earth, the sea, and the sky. *7/30/18*

Writing Topic:
List the Things I Would Tell My Parents I Am Grateful for if They Were Still Alive

1. I am grateful they picked a great little city for me and my sister to grow up in and to be able to go to kindergarten through my senior year of high school in the same town
2. Having me attend summer camp which I loved with every fiber of my being
3. Rules and freedom
4. Being taught the values of respect, integrity, honesty, hard work, and giving back
5. Their ability to laugh with each other
6. Family discussions around the dinner table
7. Letting us get a dog
8. Letting me keep the little turtle I won when I was seven years old at the annual elementary school autumn fest known as The Hallowing Ding. I named him Eddie. Later, letting me get him a turtle companion I named Ralph.
9. How playful my parents could be with each other; it made me feel secure
10. Reassuring me they were not getting divorced after nasty fights; staying together through thick and thin for sixty-seven years
11. Dinner on the table every night, always together
12. Having to do dishes and chores
13. Shopping for new school clothes every year

14. Not forcing me to eat food I did not like
15. Thanksgivings with family, my mom making all the traditional fixings, my dad's prayers and carving the turkey perfectly; my mom's post-Thanksgiving turkey soup
16. Allowing me to have three scoops of ice cream in my bowl
17. My dad teaching me how to play golf and tennis and all the life lessons he bestowed alongside them that were so much more than golf and tennis
18. My grandmother and great aunt always spending the holidays with us
19. Encouraging me to always do my best
20. Family weekend getaways in the 1960s to a nearby air-conditioned Holiday Inn to escape the heat and swim in a pool
21. My mom making the big Sunday meal after church so my dad could make us popcorn and milkshakes for Sunday-night dinners
22. My dad taking me and my sister shopping and out to dinner downtown for our birthdays; coming all the way home from work to get me and then going back again for the evening shopping spree
23. My mom's love of Christmas and making it special
24. Teaching me the values of service and giving back through their volunteer work and philanthropy
25. So many more things a list cannot possibly contain it all

Mom and Dad, thank you, thank you, thank you. *8/27/18*

Haiku 2021

Sun

the sun is there
whether we notice it or not
reliable friend

Looking Back

look back in gratitude
keep it close on your nightstand
it will wait for you

Spring Surprise

death has not arrived yet
hummingbirds still visit
sweet sweet nectar

QUESTIONS TO CONTEMPLATE

❀ What does gratitude look like to you? Is it in the moment? Does it arise from the small things or the big things?

❀ Do you have a daily practice of giving thanks?

❀ What opens your heart to gratitude?

❀ Do you think there are people, things, and circumstances in your life that you take for granted? If so, can you list three things or people you want to give thanks for right now, and then do it?

Chapter 5

LOVING-KINDNESS

"Continue
To be who and how you are
To astonish a mean world
With your acts of kindness."

—from "Continue" by Maya Angelou

Loving-kindness is a beautiful thought. What is loving-kindness exactly? We almost always recognize it when we see it or feel it. We also know when we do not. It has the capacity to open our hearts in ways we have never imagined.

It does not cost anything to give our loving-kindness. Ironically, when we give it away, we get it in return. Try it. See how you feel, especially if you are giving it to someone you really do not want to give it to.

Loving-kindness can be a simple act of listening, giving your full attention to someone without judgment. It might be allowing the woman behind you in the grocery line to go ahead of you as she juggles her cart and a crying child, even though you are tired and your feet hurt. It might be stopping to give the homeless person you pass by a hundred times some money or a snack and look them in the eye and say, "May God bless you and keep you safe."

Richard Selzer, a surgeon at Yale and also an essayist, wrote an essay called "The Kiss." I want to share it here as a beautiful example of loving-kindness.

> I stand by the bed where a young woman lies, her face post-operative. Her mouth twisted in palsy; clown-ish. A tiny twig of the facial nerve, the one to the muscles of her mouth, has been severed. She will be thus from now on. The surgeon had followed with religious fervor the curve of her flesh, I promise you that. Nevertheless, to remove the tumor in her cheek I had to cut the little nerve.

> Her young husband is in the room. He stands on the opposite side of the bed, and together they dwell in the evening lamp light. Who are they, I ask? They gaze at each other and touch one another so generously. The woman speaks, "Will my mouth always be like this," she asks. "Yes," I say, "it will. It's because the nerve was cut." She nods a silent nod. But the young man smiles. "I like it," he says. "It's kind of cute."

And all at once. I know who he is. And unaware of my presence, I lower my gaze, for one is not bold in an encounter with the gods. And then he bends to kiss her crooked mouth, and I so close I can see how he twists his own lips to accommodate to hers to show her that their kiss still works. And I remember that the gods appeared in ancient Greece as mortals, and I hold my breath and let the wonder in. There is something about the LOVING HEART that can take the measure of tears and sorrows that make up our human life, and the beauty that makes our human life and meet it in a way that is very different than any other way we would approach it.

One of the saddest things to me is when someone has been deeply hurt and their heart closes and hardens. In this hardening, they often push people, opportunities, and love away, the very things they need to heal. When I have known someone like this, I never give up giving them loving-kindness whenever I can. You never know when a tipping point may happen for them.

Etty Hillesum, a woman of Jewish faith, was born in the Netherlands in 1914. During WWII, she spent time in Westerbork Concentration Camp and ultimately was transferred to Auschwitz where she passed. In her diary, *An Interrupted Life*, she shared the unbearable atrocities of life in a concentration camp, yet again and again turns toward God and love:

The opportunity to practice loving-kindness is around us all the time. Time and again I have had to learn how spacious the heart can be, and time and again I have had to reclaim that space.

We always have the choice of practicing loving-kindness no matter what the circumstances. We can direct it toward ourselves or others. It can be a silent intention or prayer for someone. In the Buddhist tradition, loving-kindness is called metta. Metta is a practice. In practicing metta or loving-kindness, you direct 3–5 phrases toward a specific person and you repeat them for as long as you wish. As an example, those phrases might include:

"May you be safe and free from harm."
"May you be free from fear."
"May you know joy and be happy."
"May you know well-being."
"May you know peace."

When practicing metta, you practice for each person individually. You can include any number of family, friends, and beloved pets depending on how much time you have. You can expand metta to include your colleagues, community, and people you don't know but encounter, like the cashier at the grocery store. You can also extend metta to people you have unresolved issues with or do not like. As the practice expands outward, you can include your nation, refugees, other countries going through hardships, and the entire world. Metta is a simple heart-opening practice you can do anytime, anywhere.

When I learned metta while going through my mindfulness meditation teacher training program, I realized that this practice offered me something very tangible to give during the restrictions of the COVID pandemic when my immune-compromised cancer status prevented me from getting out and about.

A loving-kindness practice can be as simple as saying something kind or doing something for someone with no expectation of thanks or appreciation. You can make it your intention to practice it at least once a day. See how your life changes. We were born out of love. We return to love. In the words of Ram Dass, we can "be love now."

~ QUOTES ~

Here's to the bridge-builders, the hand-holders, the light-bringers, those extraordinary souls wrapped in ordinary lives who quietly weave threads of humanity into an inhumane world. They are the unsung heroes in a world at war with itself. They are the whisperers of hope that peace is possible. Look for them in this present darkness. Light your candle with their flame. And then go. Build bridges. Hold hands. Bring light to a dark and desperate world. Be the hero you are looking for. Peace is possible. It begins with us.

—L. R. Knost

As I walked out the door toward the gate that would lead to my freedom, I knew that if I didn't leave my bitterness and hatred behind, I'd still be in prison.

—Nelson Mandela

When you are kind to others it not only changes you, it changes the world.

—Rabbi Harold Kushner

Go where your deepest yearning meets the world's greatest need.

—Jesuit Teaching

We have to be militants for kindness, subversive for sweetness and radicals for tenderness. And then also fight for justice.

—Cornel West

~ POEMS ~

"Kindness"
by Naomi Shihab Nye

Before you know what kindness really is
You must lose things,
Feel the future dissolve in a moment
Like salt in a weakened broth.
What you have held in your hand,
What you counted and carefully saved,
All this must go so you know
How desolate the landscape can be
Between the regions of kindness . . .

Before you know kindness as the deepest thing
Inside,
You must know sorrow as the other deepest thing.
You must wake up with sorrow . . .

Then it is only kindness that makes sense
Anymore . . .
Only kindness that raises its head
From the crowd of the world to say
It is you I have been looking for,
And then goes with you everywhere
Like a shadow or a friend.

"An Interruption"
by Robert S. Foote

A boy had stopped his car
To save a turtle in the road;
I was not far

Behind, and slowed,
And stopped to watch as he began
To shoo it off into the undergrowth—

This wild reminder of an ancient past,
Lumbering to some Late Triassic bog,
Till it was just a rustle in the grass,
Till it was gone.

I hope I told him with a look
As I passed by,
How I was glad he'd stopped me there,
And what I felt for both
Of them, something I took
To be a kind of love,
And of a troubled thought
I had, for man,
Of how we ought
To let life go on where
And when it can.

PERSONAL WRITINGS

Writing Topic:
What Do I Aspire to Be More Of?

Quote Prompts

As I get older, I realize that the thing I value most is good-heart-edness.

—Alice Walker

As rain falls equally on the just and the unjust, do not burden your heart with judgment but rain your kindness equally on all.

—The Buddha

Poem Prompt

"Why I Wake Early"
by Mary Oliver

Hello, sun in my face.
Hello, you who make the morning
and spread it over the fields
and into the faces of the tulips
and the nodding morning glories,
and into the windows of, even, the
miserable and the crotchety—

best preacher that ever was,
dear star, that just happens
to be where you are in the universe
to keep us from ever-darkness,
to ease us with warm touching,
to hold us in the great hands of light—
good morning, good morning, good morning.

Watch, now, how I start the day
in happiness, in kindness.

I aspire to be more kind to myself and others. What would this look like if I lived more with intentional kindness? I would take more time to listen and listen deeply. I would inquire more before I speak or act. I would judge others less. I would find ways to be kind in every encounter. No, not just find them but become them, become the way of kindness, embody it.

I would not tense in situations where I want things to be different. I would be patient and discern when to act with purpose, whether out of anger, love, or something else. I would be kind to myself every day, eliminating unhelpful criticism and replacing it with little pep talks.

I would nourish myself. I would nourish others with love and give more freely with an open heart. When I see those who are struggling, on a street corner holding up a sign, "will work for food," instead of looking the other way or feeling some buried disdain, I will have something handy to give them, change, food, a kind smile as I look them in the eyes, followed by words such as may you be safe and blessed, so they know they are worthy of being acknowledged and do not go away empty handed to greet the long line of cars that follow me with stony faces. *7/30/18*

Writing Topic:
What Message Would You Leave for Yourself on Your Own Answering Machine?

Quote Prompt

Be kind whenever possible. It is always possible.
—The Dalai Lama.

Be gentle with yourself, Nan. Be kind, be kind, be kind. You are loved. You have loved. Be joyful and full of wonder. Wake up to every moment and live each day as if it were your last. *10/13/16*

Writing Topic:
What Am I Hungry For?

Poem Prompt

"Unison Benediction"
by May Sarton

Return to the most human,
nothing less will nourish the torn spirit,
the bewildered heart,
the angry mind:
and from the ultimate duress,
pierced with the breath of anguish,
speak of love.

Return, return to the deep sources,
nothing less will teach the stiff hands a new way to serve,
to carve into our lives the forms of tenderness
and still that ancient necessary pain preserve.

Return to the most human,
nothing less will teach the angry spirit,
the bewildered heart;
the torn mind,
to accept the whole of its duress,
and pierced with anguish . . .
at last, act for love.

What am I hungry for? This question can be answered literally or
figuratively. I am choosing to answer it literally today. What I am
hungry for is pizza. Not just any pizza, specifically Coccia House
pizza. I have flown for miles across the country back to Ohio and
driven several hours just to cross the threshold of Coccia House.

83

I learned about this pizza restaurant during my liberal arts college days in the small town of Wooster, Ohio. We worshipped this pizza and so did the locals.

Coccia House was founded in 1958 (the year I was born), in a little red house on 1st Avenue by the Coccia family from Italy. It is still run by the Coccia grandchildren today. That is sixty years of pizza.

It is so much more than great pizza. People line up like pilgrims taking healing waters an hour before it opens at 5 pm. Each pizza takes an hour to make and bake. Everyone waits, no exceptions. No one cares. You do have the option to call ahead and order your pizza and then try to time your arrival perfectly to get a table right before the pizza is ready. On rare occasions, I have timed it correctly and felt like I won a gold medal.

Coccia House is old. The floors squeak, the wallpaper is peeling at the corners. The placemats look like they are from the 1960s, plastic and reusable. This is part of its lore and charm.

In 2018, I returned for my thirty-fifth college reunion. The first night there, we ceremoniously kicked off the weekend with friends at Coccia House. A friend of mine, also flying in from California, was late. That night, I saved three pieces for him. They were wrapped in four layers of foil to stay warm. I left a note on the dorm room door where I knew he would be bunking. After midnight, I heard a knock on my door. I handed him the pizza. No words needed to be exchanged. Coccia House people get it.

The pizza is a work of art. It always comes out of the stone ovens piping hot. The smell hits you first and then the saliva starts. It is pure food joy. The cheese is five layers thick. I am not exaggerating. The tomato sauce is from locally grown tomatoes and you swear you have just bitten into one right off of the vine. The meat mixture is like no other, a secret family recipe, and you will taste it for at least twenty-four hours. The crust is divine, part dough, part pie crust, part sin.

Dive in. No regret, no guilt, pure pleasure.

Coccia House is in Wooster, Ohio, smack dab in the middle of Amish country. I live in San Diego. I have talked about this pizza with Connie since we got together in 1996. Early in our relationship when we were visiting Ohio, I knew I wanted her to have the Coccia House experience. I chose a Sunday. We made the hour-and-a-half drive to Wooster.

I had forgotten that many places in the Midwest are closed on Sundays, a long Christian tradition to honor the day of the Lord. When we pulled into the parking lot at 4:30 pm, I was shocked to not see any cars. Undaunted, I made my way to the front door. I thought we were early until I saw the "Closed" sign. I peered inside through the window. I pressed my face hard against the glass to see if I could see anything moving. I am sure my nose prints are still on Coccia House's front window. That was 1999.

Crushed, Connie and I drove back silently through the cornfields to my sister's house. For a moment it occurred to me that I may have overemphasized how great the pizza was, but I knew in my heart I had not.

On my fortieth birthday, I got home after a long day at work. It was mid-week. I smelled pizza. I thought, that is great, a perfect, easy dinner. No frills. We had a glass of wine and talked about our days. Suddenly, Connie said to me, "Why don't you check on the pizza?"

When I opened the oven there was a typical white pizza box with green and red lettering. It all hit me when I finally recognized the smell and saw the words Coccia House. I was stunned. My long-lost love had found me.

I looked at Connie, looked back at the box and carefully removed it from the oven like a fragile piece of glass. "What? How? It can't be?" "Yes, it is, it can be," she said. I was speechless. It was truly a great gift, no really, the best surprise birthday gift ever in the history of the world at the moment for me.

This pizza had flown over 2,500 miles Federal Express. It was shipped frozen. When it arrived and Connie answered the door before I got home, the Federal Express delivery woman told Connie whatever was in that box smelled so good she was hoping we would not be home so she could keep it.

Connie finally made it to Coccia House with me several times over the years. Still, the times we were able to visit there were few and far between. Fast forward to 2020, the year of the COVID pandemic and our twenty-fifth anniversary on July 17th. We were semi-quarantined and there would be no celebration or going out to dinner. I had been and was very immune-compromised due to my cancer treatments.

Unbeknownst to me, Connie was conspiring with a friend of mine from college, Cindy Weiler-Moore, who lived in Florida, to get a Coccia House pizza delivered for our anniversary. Connie and Cindy coordinated with Tom McArthur at the Wooster Alumni House and got the pizza shipped. Coccia House was only open for takeout and they had stopped shipping pizzas, so Tom had to prepare the shipping box and drive the pizza to Akron, Ohio, for mailing.

What does Coccia House pizza have to do with loving-kindness? Nothing and everything. Connie has demonstrated loving-kindness every day since we have been together. The act of getting me this specific pizza from across the country on two special occasions was loving-kindness in action. Loving-kindness has so many ways to be expressed, every day. Sometimes we forget the people right in front of us. Connie certainly did not. *5/18/16* and *2021*

Haiku 2021

Be Kind

loving-kindness matters
don't think it fluffy stuff
or it might skip you

Recipe

too much celery
eaten with an open heart
grandma's meatloaf

Hope

until the last breath
never gave up on you
red bougainvillea

QUESTIONS TO CONTEMPLATE

❀ What are the ways you practice loving-kindness in your life right now?

❀ When have you unexpectedly received loving-kindness? How did it make you feel?

❀ Can you commit to a practice of doing one act of loving-kindness a day? If not, why not?

Chapter 6

GRIEF AND SORROW

> ❝*This being human is a guest house
> every morning a new arrival.*
>
> *A joy, a depression, a meanness,
> some momentary awareness comes
> as an unexpected visitor.*
>
> *Welcome and entertain them all!
> Even if they are a crowd of sorrows,
> who violently sweep your house
> empty of its furniture,
> still, treat each guest honorably.
> He may be clearing you out for some new delight.*❞
>
> —from "The Guest House" by Rumi

Who among us has not been touched by grief and sorrow? Some of us live our lives trying to avoid it. Some of us seem to have been given an extra heaping portion of it. For sure there are days it will knock on your door.

I have learned you can try and not let grief and sorrow in, but it may enter anyway. I have also learned to sit with it. Grief and sorrow in my life has been large and small and everything in between.

Grief can sneak up on you. I remember when Connie and I lived in an area of San Diego called Mt. Helix. It was close to San Diego but felt rural and was surrounded by trees. Our property used to be part of a large avocado farm. We had a view of nature from every room.

Our front living and dining room had large picture windows, which we loved. Not long after we moved in, I heard a loud thud at the front of the house. I went out to see what it was. A bird had flown into our window. It had broken its neck and died, hopefully instantly. No matter what we did to the windows, we could not stop this from periodically happening to our little bird friends.

Each time a bird hit the window and died, my heart hurt. I felt sad and grieved over these beautiful creatures. What could I do? I could say it was silly and not feel my feelings. That did not feel right. What did feel right was to carefully and thoughtfully carry these birds to a final resting spot with love and dignity. Isn't that what we all want?

Connie and I had lived through numerous deaths of birds at the front of our house before I encountered the below poem, which beautifully captures what we felt.

"The Lead"
by Mary Oliver

Here is a story
to break your heart.
Are you willing?
This winter
the loons came to our harbor
and died, one by one,
of nothing we could see.
A friend told me
of one on the shore
that lifted its head and opened
the elegant beak and cried out
in the long, sweet savoring of its life
which, if you have heard it,
you know is a sacred thing,
and for which, if you have not heard it,
you had better hurry to where
they still sing.
And, believe me, tell no one
just where that is.
The next morning
this loon, speckled
and iridescent and with a plan
to fly home
to some hidden lake,
was dead on the shore.
I tell you this
to break your heart,
by which I mean only
that it break open and never close again
to the rest of the world.

The big griefs—death of loved ones, a marriage breaking up, abusive relationships, a serious illness, loss of a job or income— can bring us to our knees. Grief and sorrow can be all-consuming. Pain and sorrow seem to flow through our veins when the big griefs visit. We wake up hoping it was a dream and it will go away.

One of those times I was hoping it was all a dream was the day I got the "dreaded phone call" we all pray we never get. That day was May 13, 2016, when Gabriella (Gabby), my cousin Tom Park's wife, called to let me know Tom had experienced a cardiac arrest at 2 am. She had tried to resuscitate him but to no avail. Gabby is a slight woman, but she had taken CPR when her kids were in scouts. Gabby knew enough to pull Tom off the soft surface of the bed onto the floor to have a harder surface to pump against. With all the strength she could muster, and while she called 911 with one hand, she never stopped doing CPR until the paramedics arrived.

You always remember where you were when you heard "the news." Time stops. I was driving to work the morning of Gabby's call. My heart sank as she relayed what happened and that there was only a 5 percent chance Tom would live and if so, likely with major complications. His body was put on ice and his temperature cooled to 92 degrees for three days. Sorrow and anticipatory grief hit me like a lightning bolt. *I love this man*, I thought. *He can't go. Tom is like a brother to me. I have to go first.*

Tom and Gabby were in the process of moving to San Diego from L.A. and I had imagined how much more we would be able to see each other. Now, the days passed slowly with an uncertain outcome hanging over all of us like a dark, low cloud. I lived in a constant state of disbelief and sorrow. Tom's father—my uncle Bill, whom I never met—and our grandfather, Bill senior, both died of heart attacks, at thirty-nine and sixty years of age, respectively. Tom was only three years old when his father passed.

It became evident that Gabriella being trained in CPR was what not only would save Tom, but put him in the unlikely 1 percent category of not having any major complications. The day that I got the call that he had woken up and asked for a margarita, chips, and salsa, I laughed and cried at the same time. Grief and sorrow were cautiously lifting but I had intimately danced with them. Grief and sorrow had invaded my house, my soul. And now, a miraculous gift, that Tom would survive and I am happy to say, thrive.

The closer you examine the themes in this book, the more you see how they interrelate. Grief has helped me feel more connection with others, it has invited me to be more compassionate and generous, and it has taught me to increasingly live from a place of loving-kindness. It has made me more grateful for the many blessings and loved ones in my life, for I understand they may be fleeting.

I know no other way to deal with grief and sorrow but to be with it and to walk with it until I do not need to anymore. I know in our being human we cannot escape grief and sorrow. We can either let it consume us and close our hearts, or we can use it to transform our lives into being more fully human. I consciously have chosen the latter.

Because grief and sorrow penetrate our lives deeply and profoundly, I had a hard time selecting just a few poems for this chapter. All the ones I have collected over the years on this theme touched me in some way. So, with love, I share a few extra with you in hopes that when your darkest days come—and they will—these will provide you with the hope and understanding you need.

~ QUOTES ~

Grieving allows us to heal, to remember with love rather than pain. It is a sorting process. One by one you let go of the things that are gone and you mourn for them. One by one you take hold of the things that have become a part of who you are and build again.

—Rachel Naomi Remen

You will lose someone you can't live without, and your heart will be badly broken, and the bad news is that you never completely get over the loss of your beloved. But this is also the good news. They live forever in your broken heart that doesn't seal back up. And you come through. It's like having a broken leg that never heals perfectly—that still hurts when the weather gets cold, but you learn to dance with the limp.

—Anne Lamott

~ POEMS ~

"Walking North"
by Mark Nepo

No matter how I turn
the magnificent light follows.
Background to my sadness.
No matter how I lift my heart
my shadow creeps in wait behind.
Background to my joy.
No matter how fast I run
a stillness without thought is where I end.
No matter how long I sit

there's a river of motion I must rejoin.
And when I can't hold my head up
it always falls in the lap of one
who has just opened.
When I finally free myself of burden
there's always someone's heavy head
landing in my arms.
The reasons of the heart
are leaves in wind.
Stand up tall and everything
will nest in you.
We all lose and we all gain.
Dark crowds the light.
Light fills the pain.
It's a conversation with no end,
a dance with no steps,
a song with no words,
a reason too big for any mind.
No matter how I turn
the magnificence follows.

"Sonnets to Orpheus II, 29"
by Rainer Maria Rilke

Listen
Quiet friend who has come so far,

feel how your breathing makes more space around you.
Let this darkness be a bell tower
and you the bell. As you ring,

what batters you becomes your strength.
Move back and forth into the change.
What is it like, such intensity of pain?
If the drink is bitter, turn yourself to wine.

In this uncontainable night,
be the mystery at the crossroads of your senses,
the meaning discovered there.

And if the world has ceased to hear you,
say to the silent earth: I flow.
To the rushing water, speak: I am.
Let This Darkness Be a Bell Tower

"Blessing"
by John O'Donohue

On the day when
the weight deadens
on your shoulders
and you stumble,
may the clay dance
to balance you.
And when your eyes
freeze behind
the grey window
and the ghost of loss
gets in to you,
may a flock of colours,
indigo, red, green,
and azure blue
come to awaken in you
a meadow of delight.
When the canvas frays
in the currach of thought
and a stain of ocean
blackens beneath you,
may there come across the waters

a path of yellow moonlight
to bring you safely home.
May the nourishment of the earth be yours,
may the clarity of light be yours,
may the fluency of the ocean be yours,
may the protection of the ancestors be yours.
And so may a slow
wind work these words
of love around you,
an invisible cloak
to mind your life.

"The Unbroken"
by Rashani Réa

There is a brokenness
out of which comes the unbroken,
a shatteredness
out of which blooms the unshatterable.
There is a sorrow
beyond all grief which leads to joy
and a fragility
out of whose depths emerges strength.
There is a hollow space too vast for words
through which we pass with each loss,
out of whose darkness we are sanctioned into being.
There is a cry deeper than all sound
whose serrated edges cut the heart
as we break open
to the place inside which is unbreakable
and whole
while learning to sing.

"A Prayer"
by Clarissa Pinkola Estés

Refuse to fall down
If you cannot refuse to fall down,
refuse to stay down.
If you cannot refuse to stay down,
lift your heart toward heaven,
and like a hungry beggar,
ask that it be filled.
You may be pushed down.
You may be kept from rising.
But no one can keep you from lifting your heart
toward heaven
only you.
It is in the middle of misery
that so much becomes clear.
The one who says nothing good
came of this,
is not yet listening

"The Thing Is"
by Ellen Bass

to love life, to love it even
when you have no stomach for it
and everything you've held dear
crumbles like burnt paper in your hands,
your throat filled with the silt of it.
When grief sits with you, its tropical heat
thickening the air, heavy as water
more fit for gills than lungs;
when grief weights you down like your own flesh
only more of it, an obesity of grief,

you think, *How can a body withstand this?*
Then you hold life like a face
between your palms, a plain face,
no charming smile, no violet eyes,
and you say, yes, I will take you
I will love you, again.

PERSONAL WRITINGS

Writing Topic:
What Does Breaking Open Mean?

Quote Prompt

Do not be dismayed by the brokenness of the world.
All things break. And all things can be mended.
Not with time, as they say, but with intention.
So go. Love intentionally, extravagantly, unconditionally.
The broken world waits in darkness for the light that is you.

—L. R. Knost

Poem Prompt

"Wild Geese"
by Mary Oliver

You do not have to be good.
You do not have to walk on your knees

for a hundred miles through the desert, repenting.
You only have to let the soft animal of your body
    love what it loves.
Tell me about despair, yours, and I will tell you mine.
Meanwhile the world goes on.
Meanwhile the sun and the clear pebbles of the rain
are moving across the landscapes,
over the prairies and the deep trees,
the mountains and the rivers.
Meanwhile the wild geese, high in the clean blue air,
are heading home again.
Whoever you are, no matter how lonely,
the world offers itself to your imagination,
calls to you like the wild geese, harsh and exciting—
over and over announcing your place
in the family of things.

Breaking open is hard and painful. It is like giving birth, I am guessing. I remember the times I broke open—lost loves, harsh lessons, death of loved ones, the sight of anyone or any animal suffering or in pain.

Hearing someone weep or hearing myself weep has broken me open. Not crying, but deep, deep weeping from a place so ripped and raw you do not know if you will live or ever come out whole again.

I remember weeping until the tears were all out of me, from every corner and fiber of my being. Much of this centered around my journey of coming out as gay and all the rejection that happened. This was in the 1980s and 1990s. Those times were tricky. I was shunned. I was called nasty names that did not fit and I did not believe were true. They stung me to my core anyway. No matter what I shared from my heart, it was thrown in the trash. I was not to be believed. The predominant thought at that time was that I had a choice to be gay or not and clearly the only and right answer was to choose to not be gay.

I was told I was no longer worthy of being a member of my family. Their shame was palpable. I would think, I cannot shed one more tear, my heart cannot break again, but a few days, weeks, or months later it did. I knew there was love beneath this somewhere. I tried to find it and have hope.

The worst moment came when my uncle Chuck died in the mid-1980s. He was the husband of my mom's older sister, Jeanette. The call to say he had passed was from my aunt Ann who was the widow of my mom's brother, William Park. My parents had no plans to tell me about his death. I had to call Aunt Jeanette, who had just lost her husband, to find out about the memorial service. Of course I was invited, she said. I got a plane ticket from L.A. to Ohio. My cousins welcomed me. I stayed at their house.

The next day was the wake for my uncle. When I walked into the funeral home room, my aunt gave me a long hug, a hug that said you are still part of this family. My cousin Daphne pulled me aside and said she did not agree with what had happened to me and that she loved me. My grief that I had put in a jar on a shelf somewhere broke open again. This time I broke open because I was feeling loved for exactly who I was. And, it broke me open to see my uncle lying in a casket.

My uncle Chuck looked so peaceful in his red-and-black flannel shirt with the top part of his blue jeans showing. He was an accountant by day and the world's best gardener the rest of the hours of his day and weekends. There would be no dignity for this man to be in a suit and tie. He wore the uniform of what he loved the most, the land.

We don't know for sure, but in WWII Uncle Chuck parachuted behind enemy lines in France. It is where the term "take no prisoners" was real. He never talked about his service or the war. I think gardening and growing things became his therapy, his joy. He was grateful to have survived.

Uncle Chuck and Aunt Jeanette's home was on four acres in rural northern Ohio on the outskirts of Cleveland. His vegetables and fruit trees were prolific. His corn was legendary. He created his own hybrid mix of sweet corn. The rule of the house was, if it wasn't from the stalk to the boiling pot of water to the table in twenty minutes, it was not fresh. I remember it melting in my mouth and butter running down my chin. Eating it was a holy moment.

One summer I stayed with them for two weeks. My uncle had a soft spot for all living creatures. In fact, their home and land could have been the staging for the book and TV show All Creatures Great and Small. Often on his ride home from work Uncle Chuck would see an abandoned kitty by the side of the road. He would stop and put the kitty in the back seat of his car. My aunt would just sigh as she saw him come in with a new little one. He would then take the latest arrival to the barn and introduce the new member of the tribe to the twenty-something other cats he had rescued.

That summer I stayed with them, my uncle asked me if I wanted to help him feed the cats every morning. At sunrise, my uncle would get out multiple cans of Puss'n Boots cat food, Friskies dry food, and powdered milk that he would mix together on top of three large clean garbage can lids. The lids were just for this purpose. We would walk down the hill to the barn, him carrying the cat food laden lids and calling out, "Here kitties." From every corner of the yard and barn, cats would come running. He set the lids up on different hay bales and the cats would feast side by side. I still remember the soft sounds of their lapping up the food and milk, purrs filling the barn as they ate.

The following poem seems a fitting dedication for the early death of my uncle Chuck, a WWII survivor, whose hands were always full of earth and who tended to the little creatures.

"The Leaf and the Cloud"
by Mary Oliver

When loneliness comes stalking, go into the fields, consider
the orderliness of the world. Notice
something you have never noticed before,

like the tambourine sound of the snow-cricket
whose pale green body is no longer than your thumb.

Stare hard at the hummingbird, in the summer rain,
shaking the water-sparks from its wings.

Let grief be your sister, she will whether or not.
Rise up from the stump of sorrow, and be green also,
like the diligent leaves.

A lifetime isn't long enough for the beauty of this world
and the responsibilities of your life.

Scatter your flowers over the graves, and walk away.
Be good-natured and untidy in your exuberance.

In the glare of your mind, be modest.
And beholden to what is tactile, and thrilling.

Live with the beetle, and the wind.

As I entered the wake viewing line to say my final goodbye to this
man I had come to love and respect, I saw dozens of bouquets of
flowers. On my own, before I knew I could take time off of work
to come, I had sent flowers and a card. I read each and every card
attached to bouquets of flowers. I saw my humble bouquet as I got
closer to his casket. The flowers right next to the casket were an
extra-large, gorgeous arrangement. The card was signed from my
parents and my sister and her family. It specifically said each of
their names. My name was left off. My heart broke again. My mom

had no idea I sent flowers. In fact, she had no idea that I was coming. There was no interaction between us during that time.

After the service, I was glad that I had come to pay my respects and claim my space of still being part of this family. I left with a heavy heart, knowing the great divide was still alive and well with my parents.

Years went by. I never changed my weekly pattern of calling my parents on Sundays, me in California, them in Ohio, whether they answered the phone or not. I decided to love them through and despite my grief and sadness. I resolved to give to them in the ways I normally would no matter what I got back. I knew they were in pain too. I was sorry I had hurt them so deeply, yet I knew I had to live my truth.

Over time, things began to shift. My parents gained more understanding about gay people. I could feel they wanted me back in their lives. I shared with them that I was happy with my partner, our friends, my job, my extended California family, and my life. They did not argue with that. At that time, Connie and I had a Mini Schnauzer named Bailey. Christmas came and they sent us gifts including one for Bailey. It was a box full of bandanas for every month of the year. The earth had moved.

Eventually we had a full reconciliation, which started with my sister and her family. My niece, Courtney Obee, had declared she wanted a relationship with me and Connie. My sister and her family came to visit us during spring break in 1997.

Then my parents met Connie. We came to Ohio for Courtney's graduation from high school. It was then they were introduced. They were cautious at first but grew to love her. The next year, my parents were vacationing in Arizona and their time overlapped with a business trip Connie had. She brought them a big chocolate Easter bunny. That sealed the deal. Happiness and joy had replaced grief and sadness. My parents then came out to visit us and met Connie's family. It was a huge step for them, and I know it was still hard. Broken hearts were healing.

Breaking open has happened a number of times in my life. I do not think I am different than anyone else. I like to think that each time I broke open a little wider, a little fuller so that my capacity for compassion grew. Like a flower that has a tight bud, it can't give the world its full beauty and fragrance until it has broken wide open and bloomed into its magnificence. 2021

Writing Topic:
What Else has Broken You Open?

In 2000, I spent a month in India. It was beautiful, colorful, wild, and heartbreaking. Death was around every corner. The streets were filled with cars, cabs, cows, dogs, three-wheel vehicles, motorcycles, bikes, pedestrians, and overcrowded busses that looked like they would tip over any minute. It was dusty and loud. I remember Connie asking one of our cab drivers why there were no side mirrors on the vehicles. He replied that they always got knocked off. Frequent and liberal use of the horn replaced the side mirrors. Traffic rules were followed and not followed by some magical order that defied western logic.

After the first few days of being terrified every moment while on the road, I completely surrendered the driving to the capable Indian drivers. I relaxed. I never watched. But what I did see out the window sometimes delighted me and sometimes broke my heart. Beside the business of people and vehicles going every which way, there were souls on the side of the road, some begging, some suffering, some dying.

One day, I saw a man with no legs crawl by the use of his arms over to a scrap of food a plump gentleman neatly dressed had thrown to him that landed in the dirt. He scooped it up with two fingers, put it in his mouth, looked up and smiled. Tears welled up and stung my eyes. I began to silently weep. Was this the best humanity can do? Some of us with more than our share, and some simply grateful for a dirty scrap of food? It is not just India. Poverty and suffering are worldwide, it is just more out in the open there. Witnessing this broke me open in a way I have never felt before.

Maybe that is it. We cannot bloom as a human species until we all have broken open. The sight of people after a hurricane or fire has destroyed everything they have, or a child being bullied, or watching someone being shot on the nightly news, when is it enough to break us open to live differently? How much suffering do we have to hear about or see to crack our shells? Apparently, many of our shells are thick and strong.

Roshi Joan Halifax, founder of Upaya Zen Center in Santa Fe, New Mexico, wrote a book called *Being with Dying*. In it, she introduces the concept of having a "strong back and soft front" in order to be with people who are dying and suffering. To me, this concept means your spine is strong enough to be with suffering, sorrow, and grief and not turn away, but you can also witness and tend to people with a compassionate, open heart.

I think breaking open can help us lean into our humanity more. We can cultivate this capacity to have a strong back and soft front through our own suffering, letting our humanity ripen into a compassion for ourselves, others, and our planet. To me, Jesus Christ was the best example of one who lived from this place and was the Divine in human form. Perhaps we are all destined to get there too one day. 2021

Writing Topic:
When I Heard the Word "Cancer"

Quote Prompt

When you hear the word "cancer" it's as if someone took the Game of Life and tossed it into the air. All the pieces go flying. The pieces land on a new board. Everything has shifted. You don't know where to start.

—Regina Brett

When I heard the word "cancer" in 2005, sorrow and fear took over my body. The fear felt as though it came from inside me and was trying to get out, but it was captured within the walls of my skin, circulated through my blood, and took up space in my gut and lungs. My mind had nowhere to safely rest.

I did not invite cancer to take up residence in me. There was no for rent, no for lease, long or short term offered, and certainly not a for sale sign. But there it was. No words could take back what was uttered and showed up in the biopsy. No words could reverse this cancer fear and the sorrow that accompanied it.

Cancer fear does not just have one spot, it can be pervasive. Especially as I navigated the first months. For me, it was like being in a haunted house, never knowing what lurked ahead but knowing it could not be good.

Since I first heard the words "you have cancer" in 2005, I have had many reprieves, long stretches of good old-fashioned denial, and many positive and hopeful thoughts. I always believed Connie and I would grow old together, taking our last breaths sometime in our eighties.

Once the knowledge was there that cancer had entered my body, the fear never really left. Especially after it returned with a metastatic vengeance in 2014. Fear sat on my shoulder. I did my best to ignore it yet also pay attention to what it had to teach me—don't put off to tomorrow what you can do today, be willing to try a treatment, say what you need to say now, especially telling people you love them, because you don't know how many tomorrows there will be.

Fear lurked in dark corners. Being in this cancer ocean for many years, I now know how to ride its waves better. Every year since 2014, my life has been a concoction of fear, disappointment, sorrow, hopefulness, and gratefully many, many days of joy and living and loving more fully than I ever have before.

There it is, the proverbial mixed blessing. Yes, the word "cancer" combined with sorrow and fear have been constant companions. I have made friends with them, leaned into them, and been brutally honest with them, so that I can go deeper, be authentic, show my weary self and on good days, my magnificent self. *2/2/18*

Writing Topic:
Cancer the Cat, Me the Mouse

Sometimes I feel like cancer is the cat and I am the mouse. This cat, she bats me back and forth with her paws. I am trapped and filled with anxiety. I dart from here to there with no escape route possible.

Sometimes she sleeps and I rest too. Yet there is no way out. Freedom from her eludes me. She pounces sometimes when I don't expect it and traps my tail. I spin about in a circle. I swear she is laughing at me.

A Cheshire cat this one. As she looks away feigning disinterest, I seize the moment and slip my tail from under her grip. Now, cowering in a corner she can't quite reach, I can barely breathe.

This cat, she stares at me for a long time knowing she can consume me whenever she wants. My heart pounds, my mind races.

I just want to taste the little crumb of a cookie that was dropped nearby one more time.

One of my eyes watches it and the other watches her. I think to myself, you have no interest in that cookie crumb, you only crave raw meat, you savage. My fur, no longer the smooth grey mink coat, is ruffled and sticks out in funny directions from all her cat and mouse play.

My bones and muscles ache from all the acrobatics I perform in her presence. Moments of freedom are rare but when they come my thirst is quenched and I almost can forget this cancer cat and mouse game.

Daydreaming in the sun, her shadow appears. It is so much bigger than me. I know her devouring capabilities. I pray not today, this week, this month, this year will she finally end my life. Somehow, I know that when she captures me, I will surrender. I hope it is gentle, my final breath.

Maybe next lifetime I will be a cat, a kinder one than her, preferring canned cat food over a little mouse. *2/11/19*

Writing Topic:
What is Hope, How Does it Manifest?
Are there Times You Cannot Find it?

Poem Prompt

"Hiking the Anza Borrego Desert after Surgery"
by Francine Sterle

So much died here last year
but last month forced
peach-red mouths out of balding sand,
and within weeks coaxed
tiny constellations of yellow,

purple, and white into sandy flats,
along rocky dirt roads,
deep into Blair Valley, up through
Yaqui Pass, and what was once
simple misery shifted
beneath a thick covering of flowering
fiddlenecks and brittlebush,
chuparosa, ocotillo, desert tobacco.
What place to find myself
after the doctor's diagnosis
left its scar as if a cactus spine
had been dragged across my chest.
I will never be the same
knowing how effortlessly death
rests in the cells of my body,
yet with each step I am willing
to say yes to the chances I take,
to the hope no one can take from me
here in the midst of my recovery
now that I've seen what can thrive
in the bankrupt landscape of the heart.

I had always thought that Hope was a name I would have given myself if I had a choice. It is a lovely name. It has a beautiful sound to it when it rolls off your tongue.

Hope is that little light when everything else around me seems dark, when grief and sorrow overtake me. It is a little sweet sound in my mind when silence is deafening or everything is loud and clamoring and I cannot put two thoughts together. It is a sound true and clear. Hope has been a life vest to wear through challenging and uncertain times and, when I could find it, through the deepest moments of grief and sadness.

Other people inspire me with how under the direst circumstances they still have hope. Perhaps it is wired into us as human beings? Or is it something taught, or both? Perhaps it is hard wired into our DNA and into that of all creatures and nature.

The book A Tree Grows in Brooklyn comes to mind. My mom loved that book. A little green sprout comes up and grows into a tree in a crack in the concrete sidewalk. What are the odds? That speaks to me of determination, will, and hope.

What is it about human beings that we keep putting one foot in front of the other again and again? I think of our ancestors and refugees risking their lives to come to this country and start a new life despite the untold hardships. Have you ever seen a lone ant carrying a large piece of cracker fifty times its size, back to its ant home? The will to keep life going is extraordinary.

If I lose hope, I have lost something sacred and vital to life. Going through cancer and cancer treatments has tested this again and again. I just don't know how high my hope ceiling is. *10/13/16*

Vanishing Hope Transformed

Where do you put your hope when there is no room for it
   anywhere
Your heart cannot hold it
Your mind tells you it is no use
Your body weeps as it lets it go
It is like watching a kite disappear forever into the sky

Desperately you look for a new place
The shelves and cupboards are full and
there is certainly no room for it in the closets or garage

Yet, you carry this hope knowing it is a dust so light
even the slightest breeze will scatter it into a million
   unrecognizable pieces
Dreams yet to be lived, loved ones yet to be loved,
sunsets yet to behold, evaporate with every breath

Is there a place for hope to land or must I let it go
and live from a new realm, a land so foreign to me
where a voice whispers, you will die my friend
your reliable hope is of no use to you now

If I let go of hope
what else is there to hold this battered body and spirit
  together
Will I become a brittle sea shell easily broken
no longer able to recognize the self I have known for so long

I must learn about this strange barren country
Take it up like a new class
Prepare a light and handy backpack with different tools
  for the journey
I will kick and scream along this foreign boundary
  as long as I can before
I step fully into it

This new place on the horizon I never wanted to visit,
where dreams are let go of one by one
fading into the night
where do they go, where do they die
I must pivot my hope somewhere in a distant land
  beyond fear
Recognize the deep knowing that my spirit can stay strong
and true
open to the mystery and the unknowable
what do I need for this journey
where love is my true north and all things are beautiful

4/17/21

Haiku 2021

Approaching Dying

what season my death
will I cling to the bedsheets
no way to know yet

Death of a Beloved Friend

summer camping trip
car broadsided on a country road
friend never returned

Memory Awakened

smell of autumn leaves
life and death intertwined
my friend remembered

Bended Knee

grief will bring you to
your knees, a great place to bow
down and let it out

QUESTIONS TO CONTEMPLATE

❀ When grief and sorrow come to your life can you be with them? Do you walk with them? What has that looked like?

❀ Do you try and push grief and sorrow away? If so, has it worked?

❀ Have you gotten stuck and consumed by grief? What helped you the most to work through it?

❀ As painful as times of grief and sorrow can be, have they taught you anything valuable? If so, what?

Chapter 7

EQUANIMITY

> 66 *The work of the heart, the work of taking time, to listen, to live our values, to love well, is also our gift to the whole of the world. Through our inner courage, we awaken to the greatest capacity of human life, the one true human freedom: to love in the midst of all things.* 99
>
> —Jack Kornfield in *Handbook for the Heart*, edited by Richard Carlson and Benjamin Shield

"Equanimity" is not a word we hear often or use regularly. It means mental calmness, tranquility, composure, evenness of temper, especially in difficult situations. In Buddhism, it is the third sublime attitude after loving-kindness and compassion.

Going deeper into the meaning of equanimity, it is a steady knowing that life is transient. Out of that knowing springs wisdom, freedom, compassion, and love.

My dad had a lot of equanimity. He was a living example of it. I rarely remember him reacting in ways other than being calm, thoughtful, loving, and wise even in the most difficult of situations and amplified moments. Growing up, I did not know he had such equanimity or how rare it was. I had no sense of the term, but my dad displayed it again and again. He was like the steady rudder of a ship. Gullu Singh, a real estate attorney and meditation instructor, describes equanimity this way:

> The heart/mind that can direct loving-kindness in equal measure, without discrimination, toward the loved one and the stranger and the enemy, where loving-kindness is a gentle rain or a sunbeam that falls evenly on everyone, has a quality of impartiality of mind that is a cornerstone of equanimity. With this impartiality of mind, the mind, even if just for a moment, is not for or against anything. There is no struggle, no push and no pull, just resting in ease and contentment. From that place of resting, we can then move into the world and do what's needed with greater compassion and wisdom.

I am not sure if my dad came by this naturally or learned it or if it was a combination of both. I know when he was ten, he was sledding down a snowy, ice-filled street face first when a truck started to back up. No time to stop, my dad went under the truck on his sled and his scalp was sliced open in a half-circle. He ran home, blood dripping all over him. He rang the doorbell and collapsed. When my grandmother opened the door, he exclaimed, "Mom, I am dead." The doctors at the local emergency room cut off the sweater he had just received for Christmas. It was soaked in blood. It took over 100 stitches and a dozen clamps to close his skull. He almost died.

Several years later in high school, my dad contracted polio. He was coming home from a high school football game when it hit him. The house was empty. My grandparents found him on the floor beside his bed, too weak to have climbed onto it. He was bedridden for a year.

When he recovered, he came back to letter in track and basketball. Never one to turn down a challenge, and even though he was small and scrawny for his age, he relished the fact that he could even try out for the teams. He told me many times how grateful he was to have survived both of those close calls with death. He never took life for granted. I do not know how he did it, but he seemed to weave a quilt of gratitude into a life lived from a place of equanimity.

After he graduated from high school at age seventeen in 1942, my dad immediately signed up to be in the Navy. He never gave a second thought to serving his country in WWII. He was gone to boot camp by the fourth of July that year. My dad was stationed in the Pacific on Johnston Island. He was fortunate not to see direct combat. When he returned, the GI Bill paid for his college tuition.

Many people would say my dad was easygoing, and he was, but it was much deeper than that. He displayed a calmness through all the ups and downs of life. In the 1950s, he and my mom lost both of their dads and my mom's brother. My mom also had two miscarriages during this time. My mom would often say that it was my dad who got her through it.

My dad was humble and had a special abiding wisdom and a deep faith in Christian teachings. His favorite passage in the New Testament was the Sermon on the Mount and the Beatitudes. He aspired to live the qualities of the latter. He also had a framed copy of "Desiderata" by Max Ehrmann on the wall in his home office right where you entered the room. I read it many times coming to and from his office.

And, my dad was fun. He was playful. He loved to play a spontaneous game of tag. We would hit each other's arms back and forth, laughing until one of us escaped and declared the winner. He was competitive. He could make a game out of almost anything including throwing a scrunched-up piece of paper into a wastebasket. He loved sports and taught me to love and appreciate them.

He was fully human. He had these amazing qualities we looked up to, but he also was a regular guy in so many ways. At his memorial service in 2016, this was how he was remembered. At his service, it touched me to hear that, in particular, the men in our family saw him as a role model. He was a trusted advisor. It was not that he did not have strong opinions or ideas—he did—but he never got caught up in anger or in his ego. He was the best role model I can imagine in so many ways. He lived from a place of equanimity.

~ QUOTES ~

We cannot change
the way the world is,
but by opening to the world
as it is we may discover that
gentleness, decency and bravery
are available, not only to us,
but to all human beings.
—Chögyam Trungpa in Who Do We Choose to Be?
by Margaret Wheatley

There is something wonderfully bold and liberating about
saying yes to our entire imperfect and messy life.
—Tara Brach

God give us rain when we expect sun.
Give us music when we expect trouble.
Give us tears when we expect breakfast.
Give us dreams when we expect a storm.
Give us a stray dog when we expect congratulations.
God play with us, turn us sideways and around.
Amen.

—Michael Leunig

The heart that breaks open can contain the whole universe.
—Joanna Macy

Out beyond ideas of right doing and wrong doing, there is a
field, I will meet you there.

—Rumi

~ POEMS ~

"Go to the Limits of Your Longing"
by Rainer Maria Rilke

God speaks to each of us as he makes us,
then walks with us silently out of the night.

These are the words we dimly hear:

You, sent out beyond your recall,
go to the limits of your longing.
Embody me.

Flare up like a flame
and make big shadows I can move in.

Let everything happen to you: beauty and terror.
Just keep going. No feeling is final.
Don't let yourself lose me.

Nearby is the country they call life.
You will know it by its seriousness.

Give me your hand

"A Dream of Mountaineering"
by Po Chü-I

At night, in my dream, I stoutly climbed a mountain,
Going out alone with my staff of holly-wood.
A thousand crags, a hundred hundred valleys—
In my dream-journey none were unexplored
And all the while my feet never grew tired
And my step was as strong as in my young days.

Can it be that when the mind travels backward
The body also returns to its old state?
And can it be, as between body and soul,
That the body may languish, while the soul is still strong?
Soul and body—both are vanities;
Dreaming and waking—both alike unreal.
In the day my feet are palsied and tottering;
In the night my steps go striding over the hills.
As day and night are divided in equal parts—
Between the two, I *get* as much as I *lose*.

PERSONAL WRITINGS

Writing Topics:
Butterfly Migration and Letting Go

Quote Prompt

The Great Way is not difficult
for those who hold no attachment to preferences.
When the mind exists undisturbed in the Way,
there is no objection to anything in the world;
and you will walk freely and undisturbed.
> —Third Zen Ancestor Jiangzhi Sengcan, "Faith in Mind,"
> translated by Richard B. Clarke

Poem Prompt

"Saints"
by Louis Jenkins

As soon as the snow melts the grass begins to grow.

Even though the daytime high is barely above freezing, even
though

May is very like November, marsh marigolds bloom
in the swamp and the poplar trees produce a faint green
that hangs under the low clouds like a haze over the valley.

This is the way the saints live, no complaints, no suspicion,
no surprise. If it rains, carry an umbrella, if it's cold, wear
a jacket.

So many paths these topics of butterflies and letting go want to
take me down—my first thoughts migrating to a place of letting go
and lightening my load.

What a state it would be to live like the wandering sadhus of
India. They wear a simple loincloth and carry a few coins. Devoted
to the Divine, they wander, their body smeared with ashes of the
dead and their loincloth holding a sack with coins to pay for a
funeral pyre when they die so they can be burned to the very same
ash that others will wear on their foreheads as a badge of devotion
to something Greater than themselves and this life.

What is greater than living this life we are given? Does it matter if you run around in a loincloth or in a Mercedes as long as you
enjoy it, have gratitude, and are generous, loving, and kind?

I want to migrate from my judgments. All this sitting on the
bench of life, pronouncing this is good, this is bad, that is not so
good. Put down your gavel, can it all be good? Can it possibly be

that all the beauty, all the pain, all the magnificent sunsets and all the endless suffering means "this too"?

Can I let it all go and let it be? It seems to be a paradox. Can you let it go and be with it at the same time? Just how does that work? Can I want to end suffering but also let things unfold as they do? Can I take every possible treatment to rid my body of cancer and also live from a place of surrender no matter what happens and when it unfolds? Take action and let things work out as they will, not attached to the outcome? It takes a lifetime of practice to achieve equanimity.

When you get there, I hear it is a place of deep peace and understanding. That is a place worth migrating to. Fully engaged in the world but not trapped by it, not engulfed in my story.

The caterpillar to a butterfly tale. We all learned about it as children. Like most children, when I was little, I was fascinated by the transformation of a small jelly-like squishy bug into a beautiful flying creature that floats as light as the air, seemingly able to go wherever it wants without a care.

Cancer made me care. But maybe it also transformed me and brought me to a place of more equanimity, to let go of what I do not need any more. It lightened my load in a different way I did not expect. Did the caterpillar expect to become a butterfly? Wouldn't it be a miracle if we all could lessen our load so much, we could fly? Oh, I would love to fly. *3/25/19*

Writing Topic:
What Lessons Have I Learned from Cancer?

Quote Prompt

Opening to the reality of what is can shift us out of insisting that we need ideal circumstances to make us happy, and into an appreciation of the growth that is called out of us by life's trials.

—Barbara Cecil, *Coming into Your Own*

Poem Prompt

"Our Real Work"
by Wendell Berry

It may be that when we no longer know what to do
we have come to our real work,
and that when we no longer know which way to go
we have come to our real journey.
The mind that is not baffled is not employed.
The impeded stream is the one that sings.

Today, not tomorrow, love. Love despite the odds. Forgive with an open heart. Forgive myself, forgive others again and again and again until it feels complete.

Take more risks. Have I really done that? I remember clearly, on our last day of a little getaway family vacation, being on the end of that high diving board above the chlorinated blue water at the Holiday Inn in small-town Ohio, I finally made the headfirst dive, water up my nose, but I emerged triumphant in my nine-year-old body.

Jumping was easy. Diving headfirst was not. Did that define a real risk? It felt like a death wish, my feet stuck to the diving board plank wanting and not wanting to take the plunge. What is the worst that can happen?

Cancer has taught me the worst can happen and I just handled the cards I was dealt the best I could. Still waiting to tackle that cancer headfirst dive living fearlessly effortlessly laughing and crying all the way down. Or have I? *10/13/16*

Writing Topic:
What Would It Be Like to Be Free?
Make a List.

Poem Prompt

"When the Shoe Fits"
by Chuang Tzu, translated by Thomas Merton

Ch'ui the draftsman
Could draw more perfect circles freehand
Than with a compass.

His fingers brought forth
Spontaneous forms from nowhere. His mind
Was meanwhile free and without concern
With what he was doing.

No application was needed
His mind was perfectly simple
And knew no obstacle.

So, when the shoe fits
The foot is forgotten,

When the belt fits
The belly is forgotten,
When the heart is right
"For" and "against" are forgotten.

No drives, no compulsions,
No needs, no attractions:
Then your affairs
Are under control.
You are a free man.

Easy is right. Begin right
And you are easy.
Continue easy and you are right.
The right way to go easy
Is to forget the right way
And forget that the going is easy.

What would it be like to live free?
Be filled with light, be light
Be filled with laughter
No worries
Total trust
Complete surrender
Witness suffering, hold it with love, and take compassionate
action
Walk on water
Love everyone
See the complete tapestry of perfection of the Universe
Bow down in gratitude for every moment
Be able to fly
Know that I am Loving Awareness, nothing more, nothing
less

Love myself
Be joyful, be joy
Jump and skip with childlike abandon
No fear of falling, no fear of dying
Know with certainty everything is a gift
I want to know how God thinks, everything else is a detail
(Einstein)
Have the eyes of a child and the wisdom of an old sage
Judge no one
Be calm in the midst of a storm
Embody Christ Consciousness

Know in my bones what the Sufis said, "Good where we've been, good where we're going to"

Now that would be living free. *2/18/17*

Haiku 2021

Peace-Filled

in front of me
the sidewalk or the trail
it doesn't matter

Steady

is there a steady mind
that can hold all opposites
without going beyond them

QUESTIONS TO CONTEMPLATE

❁ Where have you seen equanimity?

❁ Who has best exemplified equanimity in your life?

❁ Do you think you have equanimity? If so, is it rare, occasional, or most of the time?

❁ Do you believe this is a quality worth cultivating? Why or why not?

Chapter 8

MINDFULNESS AND CELEBRATING THE MOMENTS

"*For many years, at great cost, I traveled through many countries, saw the high mountains, the oceans. The only things I did not see were the sparkling dewdrops in the grass just outside my door.*"

—Rabindranath Tagore

Mindfulness. Mindfulness of what? Don't step in dog poop? Make a complete stop at a stop sign, especially if there is a police car behind you? Watch the time so you don't over-steam your fresh vegetables? Yes, these things and so much more.

Mindfulness is a practice that can be learned through a variety of techniques. Mindfulness is essentially paying attention to this moment. It is a simple concept, but not easy to master. Mindfulness is a practice designed to help you live more in the now, not ruminating about the past or worrying about the future.

We miss a lot of life because we are in our heads, telling ourselves stories, stewing about something we cannot control, or going over the same thoughts again and again. Watch your mind for a while. See where your thoughts spend their time.

Mindfulness and mindful meditation are secular practices, but you will find most religious and spiritual traditions also have practices for them. It does not matter which tradition of mindfulness or mindfulness meditation you practice; it all leads to the same end: allowing you to live more fully in the moment and enjoy life.

I spent over two years in a mindfulness meditation teacher training program. There were 1,400 other people in the program from seventy-five countries. We were divided into groups of six for our twice-a-month meeting. We stayed with the same group for two years. We went over our weekly homework and readings, we led meditations, we gave talks, and ultimately taught two practicums and took two final exams to fulfill the requirements of graduation. It was a ton of work, but so worth the time and effort. A huge grin spanned my heart when I opened the envelope with my graduation certificate from Sounds True in partnership with the University of California Berkeley's Greater Good Science Center.

You might ask, why on earth would I spend my time learning to teach mindfulness meditation knowing I was living with metastatic cancer that could take my life at any time? I recall my oncologist saying in early 2017 that in the fall of 2016 she did not think I would make it to see 2017. I know I live on borrowed time.

The answer to that question is that I knew learning how to teach mindfulness and mindfulness meditation would help me thrive through whatever cancer would throw at me. I knew it would help me live more in the moment, enjoy what I had in front of me now, and celebrate the moments, not so caught up in the "what ifs" and dire predictions.

I also wanted to learn to teach others. I consider learning mindfulness a great gift in my life and want to share it with others. So many times, my mentor in the program would say, "It is okay not to finish, Nan." But I wanted to finish. I did not want cancer to dictate the outcome.

In the fall of 2020, I finished my second practicum in between three hospitalizations due to an infection that almost took my life. I say this not for accolades, but to share my realization that I could continue living fully while dying. In my hospital room I practiced what I had learned. I joked to myself I could write a short book entitled *Ten Ways to Practice Mindfulness from Your Hospital Room.*

I thank God every day for my group of students who stuck with me as I had to change the dates of classes several times. Without their understanding, flexibility, and support, I would have never finished. Thank you to my first group in the spring of 2020, Arleen Kagen, Laurie Wagner, Pat Libby, DeDe Smith, Barbara Britton, and Barb Bush. And to my second group in the fall of 2020 for their infinite flexibility, Irma Cota, Laura Zweckbronner, Duane MacGregor, Sandra Ulibari, Arlene Kramer, Terri LeBeau, and Mary Ann Papageorge.

So why is mindfulness so important to me? It has taught me to celebrate the moments of my life. I learned that the many moments of every day may seem small and insignificant, until I pay attention. I started taking more pauses to watch the hummingbirds at our feeder. I noticed a flowering tree in my neighborhood for the first time. Noticing more what was in front of me, I increasingly relinquished living in my head.

The more I practice mindfulness, the more I notice the exquisiteness of life. I began to realize how many things I never paid attention to before. There are little gifts that surround us every day if we know where and how to look. I noticed the intricate details of where a dog's whiskers attach to its face. I felt the softness and warmth of a scarf around my neck on a cold day. I realized how many things I never paid attention to before. Then I became aware that by practicing mindfulness, I started to slow down almost automatically. I could finally sip and truly taste a cup of hot cocoa. You can bring mindfulness to anything and everything. Imagine being present every minute of your golf game. Your score might improve.

I also have found I stop taking people and things for granted. The practices I learned shifted my perspective. I stopped judging things and people's behavior as if I had a corner on what was right. Some people I found annoying I now am amused by and find them more lovable in all their humanness.

I consider myself fortunate that I had this concept of being mindful even before going into meditation teacher training. It helped with other challenging situations, like when both of my parents passed in 2016. They were still living in Ohio. Both of them had increasing dementia. Upon visiting them, I realized my dad no longer recognized me. That was a sad day that ripped through my heart. Aunt Annie, my dad's younger sister, and my cousins Elizabeth and Catherine, along with Catherine's husband Bob, had overlapped with me for a visit. Aunt Annie asked my father about me. I was sitting next to him. He replied, "Oh, my Nan." He looked at all of us, including me, and went on to share some things as if we were strangers inquiring about his family.

Because I understood the concept of being mindful in the moment, I was able to be with my dad wherever he was in his mind, which quite often did not match where he was in time and space. When he was present, that was a gift. One afternoon, we sat together on the porch of the facility where my folks lived. He pointed out the same birds and trees to me over and over again. He loved being outside which he rarely got to do. I enjoyed watching him enjoy that.

On one particular day as we were sitting on the front porch, my dad noticed there were a lot of red cars in the parking lot and concluded they were having a sale on red cars. He told me it must be an end-of-the-year sale. He surmised one of the visitors was a salesman of the red cars.

Later that evening my dad told me about a meeting he had coming up where he had to give a presentation and he was a bit nervous. My dad was ninety-one and long retired, so of course there was no meeting coming up. I never corrected him. I just loved him exactly the way he was. It was such a gift.

The final thing I did for my dad was trim and file his fingernails. It seemed such a small thing compared to a lifetime of what he had given me. His fingernails were long and had been bothering him; the staff at his facility had not had time to trim them. I had been alternating visiting him and my mom, who at the time was in a rehabilitation facility because she had been accidently knocked down by a staff member and had broken her hip and leg in four places. Before I returned to see my dad in the evening, I ran out to Target and got what I needed for his manicure.

When I returned, I found him all alone in his wheelchair in the community TV room where a Harry Potter movie preview was looping. It was beyond annoying. While I was frustrated and angered to not find any staff around, I did not want to miss this moment with just him so I turned down the volume and gave my full attention to my dad.

I cannot describe how sweet it was to trim and file my father's nails for him. He was so pleased. Tears ran down my face as I saw how appreciative he was that I was doing this for him. He did not know me. He would point out the rough spots I had missed and I would file them smoother. What an honor to do this simple act for a man who had given me so much. I can now look back and I am so grateful I knew how to be in the moment with him. I now can celebrate those precious moments.

Very few people who have walked the earth have been able to master mindfulness in every moment. Jesus Christ and the Buddha are the ones that came the closest to this mastery. Even the Dalai Lama says he is still working on it. Learning the practices of mindfulness and mindfulness meditation in some form is worth it. I guarantee it.

~ QUOTES ~

Meditation is offering your genuine presence to yourself in every moment. It's the capacity to recognize clearly that every moment is a gift of life.
—Thich Nhat Hanh, Peace Is Every Breath

Life is best experienced with a sense of awe, wonder, and discovery. Go about life with a child's curiosity.
—Tom Gregory

One day at a time—this is enough . . . live in this present and make it so beautiful that it will be worth remembering.
—Ida Scott Taylor

Life is always now.
—Tennessee Williams

The simple things are also the most extraordinary things. And only the wise can see them.
—Paulo Coelho, The Alchemist

~ POEMS ~

"Imperfection"
by Elizabeth Carlson

I am falling in love
with my imperfections
The way I never get the sink really clean,
forget to check my oil,
lose my car in parking lots,
miss appointments I have written down,
am just a little late.

I am learning to love
the small bumps on my face
the big bump of my nose,
my hairless scalp,
chipped nail polish,
toes that overlap.

Learning to love
the open-ended mystery
of not knowing why
I am learning to fail
   to make lists,
    use my time wisely,
    read the books I should.

Instead, I practice inconsistency,
   irrationality, forgetfulness.

Probably I should
hang my clothes neatly in the closet
all the shirts together, then the pants,
send Christmas cards, or better yet

a letter telling of
my perfect family.

But I'd rather waste time
listening to the rain,
or lying underneath my cat
learning to purr.
I used to fill every moment
   with something I could
   cross off later.
Perfect was
   the laundry done and folded
   all my papers graded
   the whole truth and nothing but
Now the empty mind is what I seek
   the formless shape
   the strange off center
   sometimes fictional
   me.

"Aimless Love"
by Billy Collins

This morning as I walked along the lakeshore,
I fell in love with a wren
and later in the day with a mouse
the cat had dropped under the dining room table.

In the shadows of an autumn evening,
I fell for a seamstress
still at her machine in the tailor's window,
and later for a bowl of broth,
steam rising like smoke from a naval battle.

This is the best kind of love, I thought,
without recompense, without gifts,
or unkind words, without suspicion,
or silence on the telephone.

The love of the chestnut,
the jazz cap and one hand on the wheel.

No lust, no slam of the door—
the love of the miniature orange tree,
the clean white shirt, the hot evening shower,
the highway that cuts across Florida.

No waiting, no huffiness, or rancor—
just a twinge every now and then

for the wren who had built her nest
on a low branch overhanging the water
and for the dead mouse,
still dressed in its light brown suit.

But my heart is always propped up
in a field on its tripod,
ready for the next arrow.

After I carried the mouse by the tail
to a pile of leaves in the woods,
I found myself standing at the bathroom sink
gazing down affectionately at the soap,

so patient and soluble,
so at home in its pale green soap dish.
I could feel myself falling again
as I felt its turning in my wet hands
and caught the scent of lavender and stone.

Sanskrit Salutation to the Dawn

Listen to the salutation to the dawn,
Look to this day for it is life, the very life of life,
In its brief course lie all the verities and realities of our
existence.

The bliss of growth, the splendor of beauty,
For yesterday is but a dream and tomorrow is only a vision,
But today well spent makes every yesterday a dream
of happiness
and tomorrow a vision of hope.
Look well therefore to this day.
Such is the salutation to the dawn

PERSONAL WRITINGS

Writing Topic:
Write about the Cancer

Poem Prompt

"Be the Energy"
by Danna Faulds

Trust the energy that courses
through you. Trust - then take
surrender even deeper.
Be the energy.

Don't push anything away.
Follow each sensation back to
its source and focus your awareness
there. Be the ecstasy.

Be unafraid of consummate wonder.
Emerge so new, so vulnerable,
that you don't know
who you are.

Be the energy, and paradoxically,
be at peace. Dare to be your own
illumination, and blaze a trail across
the clear night sky like lightning.

Oh, the cancer you ask? Now it has been a companion of sorts for fourteen years. I let this companion off at the curb around 2008, three years after my initial diagnosis.

"Bye, have a good life somewhere else."

I imagined dropping this cancer off somewhere in the dusty desert, Arizona, Nevada, or Texas. Somewhere it could never find me again. But it did. Damn, it took a while to hitchhike back uninvited and attach itself to my liver and bones. That was 2014.

Now cancer, my companion again. Why do I call it companion? The common language for cancer is it is the enemy you fight and battle. I live side by side with it. It does not define me. What I mean by companion is that cancer has been part of my life, not my life in its entirety, but a part of it. Cancer has also been a teacher, a radical one. It has been in my life but most of the time I do not let it take center stage.

The side effects of treatment sometimes have dominated my world—nausea, extreme fatigue, joint, muscle, and bone pain, GI issues, neuropathy, foggy brain, and many others got my attention very quickly. While it has been a "battle" at times to get these under control, what I learned was how to pay attention to my body.

In the fall of 2020, I learned what a ten out of ten pain means. There is no "leaning into it" as I have heard said. The cramps in my intestines lasted for four hours with no relief. I heard myself moan like a wounded animal. Then the flood gates opened for two hours. Connie by my side every minute. I was humbled and depleted. I will never take pain for granted again. I know what true love is. Connie demonstrated that at my worst possible time.

Mindfulness in the midst of pain and discomfort. It has a lot of wisdom to share with me. When I slowed down and noticed what was going on, it taught me to listen to my internal voice. That internal voice helped me discern what I really needed at that moment.

When life stabilized for me after different rotations of different treatments, my focus shifted to existential questions: God, mortality, my purpose and have I lived it? I also thought about how much time I might have left and how I wanted to live it. I would think, I don't want to exit this earth until I have done . . . fill in the blank.

My cancer companion taught me to look at the world differently right out of the gate. I needed help from others and had to learn to recognize it and ask for it. I began to not take time for granted. So much kindness was coming toward me I could barely take it all in. I found I naturally wanted to reciprocate and be kind as much as possible.

Cancer also taught me to say and do things now while I still can and not put important things off until "someday" because I may not have a someday. Slowing down was the hardest thing for me. I learned to slow down a bit. I practiced taking the time to taste and enjoy my food. It was hard to master in a society of fast food. I am still working on it. I really did not slow down until I retired in 2017 but I began to have more moments of being in the now and celebrating them.

I have gotten used to this cancer companion. My medical team tells me that because I have stage 4 metastatic cancer, I really can never drop her off anywhere. So, I decided to make peace and embrace this unwelcome visitor that has taken up residence with me for so long. *2/11/19*

Writing Topic:
How Can I Never Take
an Ordinary Day for Granted?

Poem Prompt

"Otherwise"
by Jane Kenyon

It might have been otherwise. Remembering that fact takes me directly to gratitude for the ordinary, everyday things the poet Jane Kenyon celebrates in her poem "Otherwise," written shortly before she died of leukemia at age forty-seven. She wrote it knowing that things would soon be "otherwise" for her. I am very grateful for the spirit she summoned as she was dying in order to leave us this gift, these words of reminder and guidance.

I got out of bed
on two strong legs.
It might have been
otherwise. I ate
cereal, sweet
milk, ripe, flawless
peach. It might
have been otherwise.
I took the dog uphill
to the birch wood.
All morning I did
the work I love.

At noon I lay down
with my mate. It might
have been otherwise.
We ate dinner together
at a table with silver
candlesticks. It might
have been otherwise.
I slept in a bed
in a room with paintings
on the walls, and
planned another day
just like this day.
But one day, I know,
it will be otherwise.

My Love for an Ordinary Day
aka An Ode to the Coffee Beans and Coffee Server

Oh, ordinary day, it could have been otherwise, but it
wasn't. How do I never take you for granted?

Ordinary day, you start with the smell of freshly brewed
coffee lovingly prepared the night before and turned on
automatically by a little button and blue light to brew at
exactly 6:40 am.

That little button ensures you are morning-ready and then
served to me by my beloved Connie, who got up, let the dog
out, poured you into a cup, and put exactly the right amount
of half & half in that cup before walking up the stairs to
gently place you on my nightstand.

It could have been otherwise.

If this is all I ever knew or know, it is perfect. It is loving perfection in action. Coffee seeds planted, grown and

bean pods picked somewhere far from my nightstand by hard-laboring hands I will never see or know. Coffee beans packed, shipped, and transported from a long distance away making their way to me.

It could have been otherwise.

Little beans then unpacked, roasted, and ground somewhere else by many other hands to then be packaged and shipped again. Now another set of hands opens a box and puts you on a grocery store shelf. We picked you off the shelf and you came home with us to be put away in a cupboard with the teas, cocoa, flour, and sugar.

It could have been otherwise.

Oh, little ground bag of beans, you have been on a long journey to my cup. And now, as an act of love and devotion you are brought bedside to me every day by a set of gentle hands. I smell you as I sip you. What I taste is love. I know that this, the whole this, is an act of the greatest love and it could have been otherwise, but it wasn't. If this is all I ever know, then I have known divine creation and that love is all there is. 2016

Writing Topic:
The Truth about Me Is

Poem Prompt

"You Reading This Be Ready"
by William Stafford

Starting here, what do you want to remember?
How sunlight creeps along a shining floor?

What scent of old wood hovers, what softened
sound from the outside fills the air?

Will you ever bring a better gift for the world
than the breathing respect that you carry
wherever you go right now? Are you waiting
for time to show you some better thoughts?

When you turn around, starting here, lift this
new glimpse that you found; carry into evening
all that you want from this day. This interval you spent
reading or hearing this, keep it for life—

What can anyone give you greater than now,
starting here, right in this room, when you turn around?

The truth about me is that I once played the part of a polar bear.
I was nine years old. I was very shy. My third-grade teacher told
my parents at the required parent-teacher night that they should
send me to theater school to help me get over my shyness. She told
them it would greatly hold me back in life.

My parents enrolled me in Lakewood Little Theater's Children's School. Off I went every Saturday morning. No cartoons for
me anymore. I was the odd gal out at the school. All of the other
kids had talent oozing out of their pores.

Despite my inability to act in any meaningful way, shape, or
form, I was cast as a dancing polar bear in The Snow Queen in
my first year at theater school. For months we practiced our polar
bear dance steps. Unbeknownst to me, the Egyptian interlude part
of our dance number that included one hand in front flat and face
down and the other in the same position behind our back was
meant to be a comedic moment in the play.

As my dad tells it, on opening night, when the curtains boomed
open at the beginning of the third act, there I was head to toe in
a fluffy white fake fur costume, face painted white, nose and lips

painted black, perched on an iceberg. The clapping and laughter that followed was a continuous roar. I had not expected it. As the music started, I felt a push from behind from one of my fellow polar bears to get moving. The laughs never stopped.

After the play ended, there was the typical congratulations on a great show. Later that night at home, my mom told me that my dad had been doubled over laughing with tears running down his face during our polar bear dance. With all the naiveté of an uninitiated theater nine-year-old, I really was not sure if we had hit the mark or not. I was confident that my part had been important. I never forgot the moment of the roar of the crowd.

After five years of weekly theater school, I emerged changed. My third-grade teacher had been right. So many learning moments were strung together in these years of facing my fears, opening up, performing in front of crowds, and eventually having fun. I am glad my parents listened. 2021

Haiku 2021

Haiku seem especially suited for the theme of mindfulness & celebrate the moments. More of them are offered to you in this chapter.

Strawberry

surprise in my mouth
ripe red strawberry singing
heard its melody

Summer on the Turkish Coast

hot august evening
mediterranean peach
dripping down my chin

Cold Rain in San Diego

hailstones pound the yard
avocado tree stands firm
knows who she is

Christmas Cookies

crispy gingersnaps
saliva can't be contained
enjoy the moment

Pause

daylilies bloom
hummingbird territory
before and after me

Unexpected Transport

passenger side mirror
strange and wild ride
snail holding on tight

Nighttime Search

garbage can rattle
three little sets of eyes watch
mother inside

Unexpected

between sky and sea
floats to a perfect landing
feather on my foot

Sweet

orange blossoms early
as if they knew
about her impending death

Lunch

solitary cow
looking around contented
tall green grass distracts

Grammar

icicles stretch out
oh, dangling participles
along the roof line

Life and Death

dewy spider web
unceremoniously
the fly was eaten

Heat

sticky summer day
beads of sweat roll down my back
crickets hum and sing

QUESTIONS TO CONTEMPLATE

❀ Are you familiar with the concept of mindfulness? Have you heard about the practice of mindfulness meditation? What do these practices mean to you?

❀ Whether you are familiar or not, is there something or someone in your life you would like to be more aware or mindful of? Who/what is it?

❀ Do you celebrate the moments, the small things in your everyday life? List a few.

❀ Do these concepts seem like a waste of time? If so, why? If not, think of one thing you could practice.

Chapter 9

TRANSFORMATION

"We create transformative, resilient new realities by becoming transformed, resilient people."

—Krista Tippett

My personal transformation has been a long work in progress over many decades. I think that is the case for most people who embark on this journey with intention. Except for the moment of Grace I described in the introduction to this book, transformation has been more of an evolution than a revolution for me.

Needless to say, it can happen either way and generally it is some of both for most of us. Sometimes we get a wake-up call when a loud clang or a flashing neon sign gets our attention. An experience like the death of a loved one, illness, loss of a job, divorce, alcohol or drug addiction, or a tragedy in the family can be that big wake-up call—or not. Transformation can happen out of circumstances and it can also be a choice.

Transformation may come gradually and organically with growing older, gaining perspective and wisdom through years lived. Life can make us bitter or life can inspire us to continually reinvent ourselves to be the best person we can be. Either way it is a choice.

For me the moment of Grace, as I call it, was that pivotal moment in my life that changed everything. I could have chosen to ignore it, but it set me on my spiritual path. I consider this the greatest gift of my life. It was wobbly at first. There have been many zigs and zags along the way. Over the years, the consistent thread has been that I have sought out spiritual teachers and wisdom teachings, I have searched for the purpose of my life, and I have consciously worked at transforming myself to be the best human being I can be.

I believe this seeking and my desire led me, both consciously and by Divine accident, to come to work for Deepak Chopra and the Chopra Center for Wellbeing for almost five years. The paths that crossed mine at a large traditional medical center in San Diego where I worked and the few times I ran into Deepak quite unexpectedly all divinely conspired and led me to being hired to work at the Chopra Center in 1996.

I attended the first weekend seminar Deepak ever gave, in 1992 in Orange County. What I did not know at the time was that one of the medical directors I worked for, David Simon, M.D., was also there at the seminar. David was advocating with the senior leadership where we both worked, Sharp HealthCare, to bring Deepak in to start an integrative medicine program. This was almost unheard of in 1992.

The seminar I attended was called Infinite Possibilities. When I returned to work after the seminar on Monday morning, I was called to a meeting and learned my boss had resigned to take a position in another state. I was immediately made Acting Vice President of Marketing. I then went on to get the position. At thirty-five, I was the youngest vice president this 6,000-employee organization had ever had. That was living infinite possibilities.

Several years later, David Simon was working at the new Chopra Center that had split off from the medical center. David recruited me and was instrumental in me being hired there. My first role at the Chopra Center was to oversee the teacher training programs for meditation and health. My title was Director of Infinite Possibilities. A year later, I was made Executive Director for the organization.

What does this have to do with transformation, you might ask? Everything. I took a leap of faith leaving the comfort of a large organization to work for a small organization whose mission was transformation and human potential. The employees and teachers I met at the Chopra Center were phenomenal. The wisdom teachings were ever present in the midst of trying to run an organization. Despite Deepak's growing popularity, the organization had a tight budget. I learned more than I can share in this book from working there, but let me say it was a transformative time in my life. Our staff lovingly called it the "karmic microwave."

Deepak loved to invite people visiting San Diego to come to the Chopra Center. We would host a free evening program for the public where Deepak was in conversation with the guest. Our largest room could accommodate 150 people. Visitors included individuals such as Rosa Parks, scholars like Robert Thurman, authors such as Jean Houston, and Nobel Prize winners in physics and chemistry. These evenings meant I had to put in fourteen-hour days but the exposure to the teachings and wisdom of these incredible individuals was life altering.

Transforming myself and living my highest potential became a lifelong quest. From all that I learned working at the Chopra Center, I looked at life and the world differently. I had expanded my capacity and made it a priority to live from a place of compassion, loving-kindness, generosity, and gratitude whenever I could. In the words of Austrian neurologist and Holocaust survivor Viktor Frankl in his book *Yes to Life,* "The question can no longer be 'What can I expect from life?' but can now only be 'What does life expect of me? What task in life is waiting for me?'"

Indeed, my next role after the Chopra Center, working in the hospice field for fifteen years, gave me another opportunity to practice this even more. Being in the hospice field and working with people who are dying, their loved ones, and the front-line staff taking care of them is a great honor and a great responsibility. Working in the field of death and dying is life changing.

In the middle of a regular workday during that time, I got a call from a man whose wife was on our service and was dying. I don't recall him saying hello, but I do recall him screaming. He was upset that a service he believed his wife needed was being denied by their insurance company and our hospice. He was threatening and accusing everyone of anything he could think to throw at us. I simply listened. I knew he was angry and grieving. He was a man of means and was used to getting his way. I could tell he felt helpless to stop his wife's death, and indeed, he was.

Over a series of days, I worked with him and the insurance company. I dropped everything when his calls came in. He continued yelling and threatening lawsuits. Eventually, I gained a bit of his trust and we worked through the issues. He did not thank me;

I believe he had no true understanding of what hoops had been jumped through.

Two weeks later I got a call from our inpatient unit (24 beds out of the 1,000 patients we took care of at home). His wife had been admitted there and I was told he asked to see me. I walked over to the unit. The second he saw me he hugged me and sobbed in my arms for five minutes. His wife had just passed. He introduced me to his children, who were young adults. It was a moment I will never forget. Something in me shifted. I vowed to never look at anger the same way again. I witnessed the grief, fear, and humanity beneath it. This man in all his grief and anger had been my teacher.

I have heard it said that the person who dies with the most toys, wins. What can you really take to your grave? Nothing. You will be remembered by how you lived your life. I have also heard it said that people will remember not what you said but how you made them feel. I hope I have gotten better at the latter. I know that I react less and discern my responses more, whenever I can.

I seek to live loving-kindness and compassion. This is where I practice, how I transform. I aspire to live from the place that Sister Macrina Wiederkehr, author of twenty-five books, describes in *The Flowing Grace of Now*, "Looking and seeing are not the same. To see requires a deeply contemplative spirit and an open heart. To see requires learning to live awake. . . . When we begin to live awake, we will see teachers everywhere."

When I have been hurt or perceive I have been hurt, I consciously choose to give the benefit of the doubt. Not that this is always my first response or that it does not sometimes take a lot of thought and reflection, it does. I try and respond with loving-kindness. It may sound corny, but especially after living with cancer for sixteen years and metastatic breast cancer for almost seven years, and now living what might be my final year, what else can be more important that I can give back to my family, my friends, to strangers, and the world than loving-kindness?

~ QUOTES ~

Our greatest glory is not in never failing. But in rising every time we fall.

—Confucius

We either make ourselves miserable, or we make ourselves strong. The amount of work is the same.

—Carlos Castaneda

Turn your wounds into wisdom.

—Oprah Winfrey

The world is before you. And you need not take it or leave it as it was when you came in.

—James Baldwin

Life gives us choices. You either grab on with both hands and just go for it, or you sit on the sidelines.

—Christine Feehan

Only those who will risk going too far can possibly find out how far one can go.

—T. S. Eliot

There are some things we learn best in calm, and some in storm.

—Willa Cather

The goal of mature religion is to help us die before we die: die to our small self so we can find our Big Self. All major religions describe this . . . in one way or another: A false and largely self-constructed identity must be surrendered before the True Self can stand radiant and revealed . . . both good religion and good psychology agree.

—Father Richard Rohr, A Spring Within Us

The spiritual task we are given is a simple one: to attend to that inner spark of radiance, to hold vigil over it until we realize it to be our self, and to dig up and cast off all argument we have with its love.

—Adyashanti

We change the world not by what we say or do, but as a consequence of what we have become.

—David Hawkins

Holy language carries the capacity to deliver hope, to deliver the Graces, to deliver inspiration, to reignite the desire to live, to help a person understand the transformation they are going through when they are experiencing a dark night of the soul. A spiritual crisis requires its own language to carry you through. And that language is holy. It is holy because it carries with it faith and a deep profound understanding of what is unfolding within you, that you are on a journey that is governed by a legion of invisible allies, holy allies, that know exactly what you are going through and why.

—Caroline Myss

To listen is to lean in, softly, with a willingness to be changed by what we hear.

—Mark Nepo

Let the hard things in life break you. Let them affect you. Let them change you. Let these hard moments inform you. Let this pain be your teacher. The experiences of your life are trying to tell you something about yourself. Don't cop out on that. Don't run away and hide under your covers. Lean into it. What is the lesson in this wind? What is this storm trying to tell you? What will you learn if you face it with courage? With full honesty and—lean into it.

—Pema Chödrön

~ POEM ~

"Courage"
by Anne Sexton

It is in the small things we see it.
The child's first step,
as awesome as an earthquake.
The first time you rode a bike,
wallowing up the sidewalk.
The first spanking when your heart
went on a journey all alone.
When they called you crybaby
or poor or fatty or crazy
and made you into an alien,
you drank their acid and concealed it.

Later,
if you faced the death of bombs and bullets
you did not do it with a banner,
you did it with only a hat to
cover your heart.
You did not fondle the weakness inside you
though it was there.
Your courage was a small coal
that you kept swallowing.
If your buddy saved you
and died himself in so doing,
then his courage was not courage,
it was love; love as simple as shaving soap.

Later,
if you have endured a great despair,
then you did it alone,
getting a transfusion from the fire,

picking the scabs off your heart,
then wringing it out like a sock.
Next, my kinsman, you powdered your sorrow,
you gave it a back rub
and then you covered it with a blanket
and after it had slept a while
it woke to the wings of the roses
and was transformed.

Later,
when you face old age and its natural conclusion
your courage will still be shown in the little ways,
each spring will be a sword you'll sharpen,
those you love will live in a fever of love,
and you'll bargain with the calendar
and at the last moment
when death opens the back door
you'll put on your carpet slippers
and stride out.

PERSONAL WRITINGS

Writing Topic:
Where Have I Witnessed Transformation?

Quote Prompt

Be patient to all that is unresolved in your heart and try to love
the questions themselves. Live the questions now. Perhaps you
will then gradually, without noticing it, live along some distant
day into the answer.

—Rainer Maria Rilke

I remember very well the day I heard the story of a man who had been transformed. We were sitting next to each other in a waiting room. He seemed eager to tell me his story.

He shared with me that his whole life he had a disdain for immigrants, especially ones from south of our US border. He was a white-collar man and had had a good job and done well for himself. He could not overstate enough in our conversation how much he resented migrants coming across our borders and taking American jobs.

One day he learned he had significant heart issues and that he would need a transplant to live. During that time, he was frightened they would not find a heart in time to save his life. He was also terrified of the surgery. Then one day he got the call that a heart had come in that was a match for him.

The surgery was performed and it was a success. He wanted to find out who the donor was so that he could thank the family. To his great surprise, the donor was a Mexican immigrant who worked in the agricultural fields picking vegetables. This stunned him.

At first, he said, he was repulsed at the idea his heart was now that of a Mexican man. As he reflected on this more and he came back to health, he was flooded with gratitude for the gift he had been given. He began to transform his thinking about immigrants. He then was on a mission to find relatives of this man to thank them.

He was able to find his donor's family. He visited them. They cried together. He learned their story. Where there was once distrust and hatred it was being replaced by love. He made a promise to the family that his donor's children would have a chance to go to college and he would pay for it. He began a program to train and hire immigrants for higher-paying jobs. He started to enjoy socializing with a group of people he once would not even acknowledge. He saw their humanity. He had transformed through this experience.

He told me he could not hold himself from sharing his story with anyone who would listen. He was so excited he had been given life. He was excited about what he called his Mexican heart and how it had changed him for the better. It was an honor to hear his story. It left me with hope that we can all transform our ignorance and hatred into love. *2021*

Writing Topic:
How has Cancer Changed Me?

Poem Prompt

"I Want to Age Like Sea Glass"
by Bernadette Noll

I want to age like sea glass.
Smoothed by tides,
but not broken.
I want my hard edges to soften.
I want to ride the waves
and go with the flow.
I want to catch a wave
and let it carry me
to where I belong.
I want to be picked up
and held gently by
those who delight in my
well earned patina and
appreciate the changes I went
through to achieve that beauty.
I want to enjoy the journey
and always remember that if

you give the ocean something
breakable it will turn it into
something beautiful.
I want to age like sea glass.

Cancer has changed me, let me count the ways.

It has brought me to my knees with pain and side effects too numerous to list. It has offered me the opportunity to face my mortality and ask the perennial existential questions that, if we are lucky in this lifetime, we do ask ourselves. It has brought me closer to my beloved Connie, appreciating her more than words can express and she will probably ever know, although I hope she will one day.

Cancer has brought me new friendships and new ways to look at life and my priorities. I have learned to have gratitude for the time I have had on this earth and for each day I have left.

Cancer has given me more questions than answers and that feels good and right.

Cancer has given me permission to call a spade a spade and to sniff out imposters and bullshit.

Cancer has given me the knowledge that I have a nicely shaped head. Losing my hair (now five times), I appreciate that fact.

All that cancer has given me, whether the gifts were welcome or not, has shaped me into the person I am today. I pray that person I have become is wiser, stronger in Spirit, and more compassionate and kinder. And, that I still know how to play and laugh with abandon.

I wonder if I am transformed enough that when I take my last breath, I do not cling to the bedsheets and try to take them with me? I hope the transformation has me going out in a burst of beautiful light, smiling, laughing, and knowing pure joy, pure love. *2/11/19*

Writing Topic:
I Will Never Be the Same

Quote Prompt

And once the storm is over, you won't remember how you made it through, how you managed to survive. You won't even be sure, whether the storm is really over. But one thing is certain. When you come out of the storm, you won't be the same person who walked in. That's what this storm's all about.

—Haruki Murakami, *Kafka on the Shore*

I will never be the same since that day in February 2005 and then again in June 2014 when I first heard the words "you have cancer" and then "it has metastasized."

Sometimes the realization of this diagnosis has been crystal clear and sometimes murky as a mud puddle. I slide back into routines ignoring it, hoping to normalize my life back to the way it was and this cancer thing will go away. Thinking and hoping against all odds that my homegrown denial will magically keep cancer at bay and it will behave itself.

But there truly has been no going back. I have learned to not give cancer that much power. I have tried to let cancer and cancer treatments take front and center only when absolutely necessary. Mostly, I live side by side with it.

Some days when I have been read the prognostic tea leaves, the reality of it haunts me. On those days, a deep sadness drips over me like a dark, thick, sticky molasses entering every pore, permeating every fiber and cell of my being. No matter how hard I try, I cannot get it off.

Yet, there is a paradox in never being the same. I have a new-found freedom to live differently, shedding old thoughts and patterns and things that don't serve me or serve humanity. Is this the ticket to my life? It may be shorter, in fact, odds are it definitely will be, but it also invites me to transform that thought of "never be the same" into the most wonderful open-armed "Yes" to life I can be. *10/13/16*

Writing Topic:
Before Cancer, After Cancer

Before Cancer	After Cancer
I was mortal	I am really mortal
I never looked death in the face	I look death in the face
I never thought about my memorial service	Once in a while I think about it
I thought I knew compassion	My capacity for compassion has exploded
I could be cavalier and light-hearted	My heart knows heaviness
I could only guess what it means to live free	Freedom has its price
I did not really know physical pain	I have been intimate with physical pain
I loved	I love more deeply
I cared about what people thought	I don't care so much
I did not have much awareness of time passing	I am acutely aware of time passing
I did not know what it felt like to be stared at	I know what it is like to be different, no hair, no eyebrows, no eyelashes, pale face puffed up on steroids, people looking away
I gave love more easily than I received it	I receive love more openly and I am grateful
I did not like pink	I still don't like pink
I was whole	I am whole and asymmetrical

2/18/17

Haiku 2021

Melting

icicles dangle
beautiful impermanence
crystals changing forms

Question

charlatan or fierce
teacher, oh why did you come
this cancer in me

Rhythm

effortlessly
seasons change and move along
sit back and watch the show

Being Born

robin's speckled blue egg
patient effort cracks open
a beak pointing out

Whirling Dervish

danced at death's threshold
more than once on the hot coals
transformation has a price

QUESTIONS TO CONTEMPLATE

❀ Have you had a moment or moments in your life you would describe as a transformation? What sparked it?

❀ If you made changes in your behavior or outlook, what were they and have you maintained them?

❀ Is transformation, living your highest potential, important to you? If so, why? If not, why not?

Chapter 10

GIVE LOVE,
RECEIVE LOVE

"What is done in love, is done well."

—Vincent van Gogh

Give love, receive love. If life could boil down to one thing, perhaps this is the most fundamental aspect of being fully human. When I found quotes for this concept, I found almost all of them included many of the other themes from this book. They could not be separated.

How did I come upon this phrase? It is not one you hear very much. When I was first diagnosed with breast cancer in 2005, Hari Hari Ramji (Baba), a teacher of mine from India who has a center in Sonoma, California, wrote me an email. At the time he sent me the email, I was scared and living with the shock that I had cancer.

What he said in the email was, "Give love, receive love. Now is the time for you to receive love." It startled me. His words were profound and prophetic. It was not a way I had ever considered looking at my diagnosis. Connie lovingly copied the messages from his email, including this one, and printed them on bright orange paper and taped them all over our house as daily reminders.

As I started to contemplate his words, that is how I saw and felt the world around me. From the doctors, nurses, pharmacy, other staff, and family and friends to the chemotherapy itself, I looked at it all as receiving love. It was a great comfort. I had a paradigm shift. I never stopped wanting and hoping I would go into full remission and that the cancer would be wiped out, but I was able to shift from living mostly in a fear space to one that could see the love coming toward me. I let it in. It became easy to give love and receive love in new ways.

Most of us, if we are blessed, have siblings. I was blessed to have an older sister, Janine, who I shared a story about in the chapter on compassion. Most people would say we are very different, but we have been lucky that we have gotten along for most of our lives. There is no one in the world who can make me laugh more than my sister.

We have had some rough patches along the way, as all siblings do. One time in particular involved emails. My sister is not especially enthralled by technology. It had not been common for her to copy people on emails, although at times she would send a group email to close family. I began noticing that Connie was left out of these group emails so I would forward Janine's emails to Connie.

I do not know why but I never directly requested her to copy Connie when sending the family emails. Connie and I had been together over twenty years at the time this happened. I believe I assumed Janine would naturally start doing it. One day after receiving an email from her with Connie not included, I reacted. I fired off an email to her. It was not a long email, but I am sure she could tell I was hurt and disappointed. I made a direct request for her to always include Connie in the future.

I have learned it rarely goes well when you send an email in a heated moment. My sister's response was not what I expected. She took what I said and expanded it to places and thoughts that had never occurred to me. The gist of her email back was that now she knew what I really thought of her. Of course, those were not my thoughts at all.

I reacted again to her second email, but this time I gave it what I like to call grace and space. I gave myself time to think through what had happened, what I really wanted to say, and how I could do it with love. What I wrote her back was that I had not meant what she had concluded from my email. I also owned my reaction. Then I wrote a long list of all the things I admired and loved about her. It was not hard to do because there are so many things I love and admire about her. As you might imagine, her email back had an entirely different feel.

"Together"
by Rosemerry Wahtola Trommer

It can happen anywhere
on this small blue and green planet—
anywhere two people co-exist,

the invitation to be generous,
thoughtful, to think of new ways
to be good to each other.
Each kindness a bridge that spans
the world's flaws. Each moment,
another chance to build another bridge.

Deep down, I knew to give love is to receive love. I am not sure this is what I was consciously thinking when this incident with my sister happened, but I knew I wanted to send her a loving, honest response. Connie is now always included in group emails and my sister is slowly embracing more technology.

Give love, receive love is the way I want to be in the world. There is a beautiful reciprocity and rhythm to it. I am so very fortunate to have had this teaching from Baba and to put it into practice in my life.

~ QUOTES ~

True peace will come only when every individual finds peace within himself; when we have all vanquished and transformed our hatred for our fellow human beings . . . even into love one day, although perhaps that is asking too much. It is, however, the only solution.
  —*Etty Hillesum, An Interrupted Life*

Love intentionally, extravagantly, unconditionally. The broken world waits in darkness for the light that is you.
  —*L. R. Knost*

Instead of seeking love, seek and find all the barriers we have created from it. And embrace them.
  —*Helen Schucman, A Course in Miracles*

We will be known forever by the tracks we leave.
                                    —Dakota Indian Proverb

Don't judge each day by the harvest you reap, but by the seeds that you plant.
                                    —Robert Louis Stevenson

Great opportunities to help others seldom come, but small ones surround us every day.
                                    —Sally Koch

You pray for the hungry. Then you feed them. That's how prayer works.
                                    —Pope Francis

Laugh as often as possible. You must. Because the world will offer you every reason to weep. So, as often as possible, you laugh. That, I think, is part of the Great Love.
                                    —Maya Angelou

~ POEMS ~

"When I Am among the Trees"
by Mary Oliver

When I am among the trees,
especially the willows and the honey locust,
equally the beech, the oaks and the pines,
they give off such hints of gladness.
I would almost say that they save me, and daily.

I am so distant from the hope of myself,
in which I have goodness, discernment,
and never hurry through the world
but walk slowly, and bow often.

Around me the trees stir in their leaves
and call out, "Stay awhile."
The light flows from their branches.

And they call again, "It's simple," they say,
"and you too have come
into the world to do this, to go easy, to be filled
with light and to shine."

"This Is What I Have to Say to You"
by Danna Faulds

This is what I have to say to you . . .
Live as if the earth exhales blessings in your direction,
As if trees speak their deepest secrets
In your ear,
As if bird songs can lift you outside your
Ordinary state of mind and bring you into truth.
Be the creative juice flowing through the universe.
Be compassion in action and wholeness in motion.
Be silence and stillness, the ocean of love so
Palpable that not one cell of you disputes the truth
That you are love.
Be so open to your destiny that it
Unfurls like a banner in the sky, a sign saying,
"Live with gratitude, generosity, and grace."

PERSONAL WRITINGS

Writing Topic:
What is One Wish I Have?

Quote Prompt

The most authentic thing about us is our capacity to create, to overcome, to endure, to transform, to love and to be greater than our suffering.

—Ben Okri, Nigerian poet and novelist

I wish to die awake. When Buddha was asked before he died, "Who are you? Are you enlightened?" He replied, or so it is said, he replied, "I am awake."

As I interpret and understand this, being awake means you are leaving this body at the highest level of consciousness possible for a human being. You can come back again as a bodhisattva, someone whose life is dedicated to helping others awaken. Taking a vow as a bodhisattva, you come back again and again until all beings are awakened. It would be an honor to be a bodhisattva. I aspire to be one.

I am a long way from being awake, but if I had one wish, I would wish to die awake.

For the rest of it, I hope Connie and my family and friends know how much I love them and how much I felt loved by them. It has been a great ride. The best E-ticket ever. *9/29/16*

Writing Topic:
Finding Love

Quote Prompt

Accept yourself unconditionally and you will recognize that everyone is part of you. Accept yourself unconditionally and there will be no one you do not love.

—Tom Carpenter, *Let Love Find You*

Poem Prompt

"Finding God at Monteflore Hospital"
by Lorraine Ryan

I remember the rhythm of the dunking;
The mop going into the pail
Juan squeezing the mop
The mop hitting the floor with a swoosh.
A ritual of three steps—
like bells at the consecration
of the Mass at St. Patrick's Cathedral.
Pine and ammonia rose like incense.

With every move, he looked up:
"How is it really going?"
"Did your boy come today?"
"How is he doing without you at home?"

Sometimes I could not lift my head
off the pillow—
when vomiting and mouth sores
wouldn't let me speak—

the swish of his mop
bestowed the final blessing
of the night.

This poem moved me. It moved me because often it is the simplest things at the right time that are the greatest acts of love. Do I notice love when it comes my way even if it is disguised as someone pushing a mop?

If life is a school, what am I supposed to learn? And, if I do not pass, do I have to repeat and come back again to learn it?

A wise teacher once told me life is about giving and receiving love. He is affectionately called Baba and he oversees a yogic retreat center in Sonoma California. I have known him for over fifteen years. He shared this concept with me upon my first diagnosis of breast cancer in 2005.

Give love, receive love, a simple concept, but not so easy to consistently practice.

Where have I done this in my life? There are the easy examples. But there are also many times I was too caught up in my drama and my story to recognize love let alone give it.

I would love to wake up and give love like the janitor in the poem about Monteflore Hospital.

Where do I receive love? Every moment of every day, breathing and walking, all of it. Receiving love has so many clever disguises, I forget.

Where and when have I not given love? I know when I have been stingy, but also know I have missed the mark unknowingly. Give me the right lenses so I can see and do better. *9/20/16*

Haiku 2021

Reciprocity

fresh-cut orange lilies
who will trim the soggy stems
twenty-five years my job

Dad

like my dad
always sharing articles
he lives thru me

Fruit of Love

tending the tree
apples bursting with flavor
this love back and forth

QUESTIONS TO CONTEMPLATE

❀ Is the concept of give love, receive love new for you?

❀ Is it easier for you to give love, receive love, or do both? If it is easier for you to give love, do you think in allowing others to give you love you have actually given to them?

❀ Is there anyone you know that you could not give love to? If so, why?

Chapter 11

LIVE AS IF EVERYTHING IS A MIRACLE

In the vastness of the out-rushing cosmos,
you are but tiny—a warm and pulsing spark.
Against all odds, your birth a brief awakening
from silent eons spent sleeping in the dark.
When you feel your heart swell with wild wonder
at the dazzling diamond chandeliers of night,
know your body was built from ancient stardust
and the universe now sees through your eyes.
So let the breath of sweet gratitude fill you,
as the light of each new day begins.
For this moment itself is a miracle,
and to live it is your privilege my friend.

—"A Brief Awakening" by John Mark Green

Live as if everything is a miracle. Think about that. Albert Einstein said, "Everything is a miracle or nothing is." What if it is true? What in his research led him to this conclusion?

For centuries, humans believed that science and religion were diametrically opposed. Some people still do. Today, the most advanced science, quantum physics, can prove there is a God, a Universal Mind, or whatever name you want to give it.

I have learned and I believe that to be born and survive in a human body is a miracle. We often refer to it as the miracle of birth. What God Mind created the daisy, pistachios, penguins, the smell of sweet jasmine, and the wind? What about the first time you tasted ice cream? Some would call that a miracle.

If I can believe everything is a miracle and live from that place, how different would my life be? How differently would I view our world and everything and everyone in it? This has been a hard concept for me to grasp, but I return to contemplate it again and again. This quote from Will Durant sums it up well: "If we have never been amazed by the very fact that we exist, we are squandering the greatest fact of all."

I sometimes think about this concept of live as if everything is a miracle. A simple example from living in a large city is when I was delayed leaving my house and passed a bad car accident, realizing that if I had left ten minutes earlier I might have been in that accident. Was that delay a miracle by design or an accident? What about the people who died or were injured? Would they call it a miracle?

Albert Einstein also said, "I want to know how God thinks, everything else is a detail." This seems to be the mystery to it all. It can all be a miracle and I could see that clearly if I had the eyes of God. To see with the eyes of the Divine, we would know it is all love.

If all creation is the Divine, then I'm walking in God, and I'm sitting in God. There's no place the Divine is not. I am always in that light. I simply can't see it, because I'm not on that level to see that light. But it's all around me. I live in that. I dwell in that truth. . . . And so, when I say "Give me some help here," I just assume from that moment that everything is now helping me.

—Caroline Myss

I still struggle with this concept but I think about it. As I approach what could be my last months or year on this earth, I ask myself, can I accept this as a miracle from Divine Love? I find myself living from two perspectives. One perspective is that I am fully human, wanting to be fully engaged, living and thriving as long as I can. The other perspective is that I'm still fully human, but trusting in something so much greater than myself. It is a bit unsteady, but I am willing to surrender, trust, and embrace the concept that we all leave this earth at the right time.

As I have contemplated the idea of living as if everything is a miracle, I see more miracles around me. It is a great place to be.

~ QUOTES ~

An authentic life is the most personal form of worship. Everyday life has become my prayer.

—Sarah Ban Breathnach

Do not feel lonely, the entire universe is inside you.

—Rumi

You are . . . awareness, disguised as a person.

—Eckhart Tolle

Follow what you love and it will take you where you want to go.

—Natalie Goldberg

Kids: they dance before they learn there is anything that isn't music.
　　　　　　　　　　　　　　　　　—William Stafford

There is nothing that occurs that cannot bring us closer to God.
Everything that happens can be an invitation to discover truth.
　　　　　　　　　　　　　　　　　—Ellen Grace O'Brian

Don't move the way fear makes you move. Move the way love
makes you move.
　　　　　　　　　　　　　　　　　　　　　—Rumi

The most incredible thing about miracles is that they happen.
　　　　　　　　　　　　　　　　　—G. K. Chesterson

~ POEM ~

"Call Off the Search"
by Robert Hall

I walk upstairs.
I walk downstairs.
I wander into the kitchen
and look through a doorway into
the living room with all its books
and oriental carpets, but I can't
find the point of it all,
can't reach into what I'm looking
for until I sit down in the corner,
pull my blanket over my head,
close my eyes, look into the
interior rooms and listen for what
is moving in there, and again be
amazed that there is a river,
constant and uncreated, flowing,

announcing itself with the sound
of life everlasting, bursting into
this wrinkled brain substance,
translating itself into muscle,
bone, fat, connective tissue and dreams.

When I bathe in that immediacy,
I never have to search for
anything again.

PERSONAL WRITINGS

Writing Topic:
How Do You Get through Hard Times?

Quote Prompt

If God gets into your soul for just a second, that's enough for a
lifetime.

—Teresa of Ávila

Poem Prompt

"Starlings in Winter"
by Mary Oliver

Chunky and noisy,
but with stars in their black feathers,
they spring from the telephone wire
and instantly

they are acrobats
in the freezing wind.

And now, in the theater of air,
they swing over buildings,

dipping and rising;
they float like one stippled star
that opens,
becomes for a moment fragmented,

then closes again;
and you watch
and you try
but you simply can't imagine

how they do it
with no articulated instruction, no pause,
only the silent confirmation
that they are this notable thing,

this wheel of many parts, that can rise and spin
over and over again,
full of gorgeous life.

Ah, world, what lessons you prepare for us,
even in the leafless winter,
even in the ashy city.
I am thinking now
of grief, and of getting past it;

I feel my boots
trying to leave the ground,
I feel my heart
pumping hard. I want

to think again of dangerous and noble things.
I want to be light and frolicsome.
I want to be improbable beautiful and afraid of nothing,
as though I had wings.

How do I get through hard times? Humor and grit are at the top of my list. Humor has many healing properties. And getting through hard times has required not taking myself or my story too seriously. Not that I do not believe in being a responsible human being, I just think the whole thing, the entire universe from the beginning, the "Big Bang" or whatever it was, seems to me one ginormous scavenger hunt. And it takes a lot of grit to live this human life, especially with a life-limiting disease such as cancer.

We humans, whether we got here through evolution or the Garden of Eden or both, are thrown clues, little ones like pink rose petals and big ones like cancer.

Look over here, where is here? Nowhere. Everywhere. None of it is linear. Getting through hard times has required a paradigm shift, a big pivot in my thinking. I realized I was not going to find any real answers through my rational mind.

It was that unspoken luminous glimpse I was given as a young girl, that it is all okay, despite the drama, the pain, the suffering, and the hard times, it is all okay. Not that this viewpoint gives me permission to walk away from the suffering of myself and others, quite the opposite. It requires compassionate action.

When I see and feel the suffering of others, my rational mind sometimes leads me to the thought there must be a cruel God or a cosmic joke. My Mind beyond my mind has given me a sneak peek that it is all so much more magnificent, intricate, and all-encompassing than we can ever imagine. Thornton Wilder captured this feeling in his play Our Town when Emily, one of the main characters who died and comes back to visit her town, Grover's Corners, says, "Oh, earth, you're too wonderful for anybody to realize you. Do any human beings ever realize life while they live it—every, every minute?"

If you are lucky, in this lifetime you get a sneak peek of the big ALL IS LOVE movie. Then you can see the miracle in everyday things. I have had this sneak peek several times. The white light when I was twelve opened the door, and cancer since I was forty-six has hammered it home. I had it during a Nine Gates Mystery School exercise when a spontaneous laughter rose up through me. I did not stop laughing for ten minutes. It was not me laughing but the universe laughing through me. I felt light as a feather. Having these glimpses of the Divine Love so strong they are unmistakable has made me want to share them with others. This is not something you can buy or earn. It is a free gift. We just need the eyes to see it.

This Divine cosmic scavenger hunt is tricky. I believe we will all get there eventually. We will all attain Christ Consciousness; it is a matter of how many lifetimes. When we do, we will fall into each other's arms laughing and crying, knowing we are all One. It is not some corny phrase. I had a great ride. Let's do it again. *7/16/18*

Writing Topic:
After Cancer

Quote Prompt

Everything that happens is the message . . .

—William Stafford

Poem Prompt

"Before and After"
by Karin B. Miller

I remember water
touching my body differently
as, still whole, I lay in that last hot bath.

now I discover a freckle
beneath where my breast once was
and feel a newness come over me.

I ask god to tell me how he loves me
and he answers
through the taste of a sweet summer peach.

water pours over a scarred, curve less mass, and
I am cleansed

After cancer I am mortal. I wonder is it really a gift and a miracle to be born in this human form? Have I wasted it? Is there time to make up for lost time?

Is everything exactly as it should be, as that voice spoke to me so many years ago when I was twelve? Can I live as if everything is a miracle? Can I hold a universe that big, that perfect, in my little consciousness?

After cancer I vow not to beat myself up. After all I have been the dutiful daughter, family-appointed mediator, work to the bone to prove yourself worthy, all-around smiles and peacemaker.

After cancer can I let my inner bitch come out to play in the right proportion at the right time? It might just be what saves me and gives me more time to be a beautifully unbounded mortal.

Can I transform into my highest potential before I pass from this world? What is that? Is there time? Does it matter? At this stage a cure or a permanent remission from cancer would be a miracle.

The potential for death from cancer is high. Can I banish cancer by taking the right treatments combined with living from a place of higher consciousness and the right thoughts? Do I need to make it a friend or my teacher? That seems absurd. What is the right path or is there no path here? Can I open my eyes wide enough to see all the miracles anyway? *9/15/16*

Haiku 2021

Divine

one divine spring evening
the universe laughed through me
it was glorious

Three Years Old

watching my father
pulling carrots from the earth
I knew miracles

Bursting

tulips popping up
speaking of miracles
fools look around you

QUESTIONS TO CONTEMPLATE

- Have you seen miracles in your life or the lives of others? What were they?

- If you experienced a miracle, how do you think it happened or where do you think it came from?

- Can you contemplate living from a place where everything is a miracle? If so, why; if not, why not?

Chapter 12

FORGIVENESS AND GRACE

“ *For us to transform as a society, we have to*
allow ourselves to be transformed as individuals.
And for us to be transformed . . . we have to allow
for the incompleteness of any of our truths and
a real forgiveness for the complexity of human beings. ”

—Reverend Angel Kyodo Williams

Forgiveness is a complex concept and can be a difficult practice for many people. Most of us can forgive or at least forget the little transgressions that have hurt us. The things we consider big hurts—betrayals, shattered trust, etc.—can be the things we hold on to for years. These then can turn into long-term resentments, and we get stuck or harbor thoughts of retribution as the only way to move on. That does not work.

The hurt we experience may be so deep we do not know where or how to start. What happened may seem unforgivable to us. The person we need to forgive may no longer be in our lives. We sometimes falsely believe if we forgive that person, we are condoning the behavior that occurred. We also may have had a part in what happened and are not able to forgive ourselves.

Why is it hard to forgive ourselves? For some of us it necessitates a need to be radically honest and revisit something we do not want to remember or have some shame around. When we avoid self-forgiveness, it festers. The need to address it does not go away.

How do we truly forgive ourselves and others? What does it look like? What is it? Forgiveness is a deliberate act to release ourselves or others from harm they have done or hurt they have caused. Feelings of resentment are released. Forgiveness does not mean excusing, forgetting, or condoning the behavior that occurred.

Forgiveness requires you to look at your anger and pain and choose to let it go. Forgiveness helps you heal your wounds. It reduces stress and mental and emotional anguish. Forgiveness means letting go of where you are stuck.

When you forgive, paradoxically, it is mostly for you. You do not have to do it in person, but you do need to do it completely.

Jesus, dying on the cross, is famously quoted as saying of those that crucified him, "Forgive them, for they know not what they do." His statement is understood as one of the ultimate acts, if not *the* ultimate act and example, of forgiveness.

One of the most profound examples of forgiveness I have heard about in my life is the story of Azim Khamisa and his son, Tariq. Azim and his family immigrated from Iran through Canada to the United States. Azim believed this country would offer the best opportunity for his son and daughter. He was thrilled when they settled in San Diego. Then in 1995, his son Tariq was killed in a senseless act of violence.

Tariq was murdered when he was eighteen years old. At that time, Tariq was a student at San Diego State University. For extra money, he delivered pizzas. Connie and I lived less than three miles from the pizza place where Tariq worked.

One Saturday night, Tariq volunteered to make the last pizza delivery of the night. What he did not know was that waiting for him was a group of gang members who did not intend to pay for the pizza. That night they were initiating Tony Hicks, a fourteen-year-old boy, as a new gang member. Tony's instructions were, if the pizza delivery guy insisted on them paying for the pizza, he was to shoot him. Tariq insisted on being paid. Tony followed his instructions and shot and killed Tariq.

Azim's grief and anger at his son's murder were all consuming. He could only think of retribution and punishment. As time went on, however, he learned more about his son's killer. He was struck that it was a fourteen-year-old boy who had committed this act. He learned Tony's story. Azim found out about the gang initiation the night his son died. Azim also learned Tony's parents were not around and he was being raised by his grandfather, Ples Felix, who was doing everything in his power to give Tony the best upbringing he could.

After his trial, Tony was the youngest person ever to be sentenced as an adult in California. His sentence was twenty-five years to life in prison. While this would never bring Tariq back, Azim realized that two young men's lives had been destroyed. "From the onset, I saw victims on both ends of the gun. I will mourn Tariq's death for the rest of my life. Now, however, my grief has been transformed into a powerful commitment to change. Change is urgently needed in a society where children kill children."

Azim decided to leave his high-paying finance job and start a foundation. He reached out to Ples and together they started the Tariq Khamisa Foundation (TKF) to offer programs to young people, especially those at high risk, about non-violence.

Father Richard Rohr describes the transformative power of forgiveness: "All great spirituality is about what we do with our pain. If we do not transform our pain, we will transmit it to those around."

Azim forgave Tony and began visiting him in prison. Azim promised Tony he would have a job with the foundation when he was released from prison. This is the power of forgiveness. Forgiveness of someone and something that happened that seems unforgivable. Instead of two lives being lost, Azim through his ability to forgive created something lasting to honor the memory of his son.

Sometime in the early 2000s, I went to a seminar where I heard Azim speak. He was getting an award for his work in peace and non-violence. When he told the story of Tariq's murder, everyone in the audience cried. Azim's story deeply moved me. I could never look at life and forgiveness in the same way again.

A couple of years later, I was taking a Southwest Airlines flight from San Diego to Oakland to attend a meeting of a not-for-profit board I was serving on. I had a window seat. All the aisle and window seats were full. A man sat next to me. I looked over to say hello and to my amazement it was Azim Khamisa, the man I heard speak at the conference.

We talked the entire flight about what TKF was doing and how many young people they were reaching with Tariq and Tony's story. It was inspiring for me to be sitting next to this man who, in his forgiveness, had transformed his life. There are no accidents. Now, here I am telling his story of how forgiveness transforms lives in my book.

An update on Azim, Ples, and Tony in 2021: In 2010, the TKF created a new program, CANEI (Constant and Never Ending

Improvement). It is offered in eight major US cities. Over the last five years the CANEI program has successfully turned around 70 percent of the youth offenders referred to the program by the juvenile justice agencies. This is compared to the state systems where the recidivism rates are higher than 80 percent. CANEI is able to make an impact at 10 percent of the cost of incarceration.

Tony was released on parole in January 2020, twenty-five years after killing Tariq. He now lives with his grandfather Ples. He has worked in a grocery store as he transitions back to civilian life and is training to be a speaker for TKF. Tony has a special and ongoing relationship with Azim and his family, all based on Azim's capacity to forgive and transform his pain.

~ QUOTES ~

All the ups and downs are grace in different wrappings, sent to refine consciousness. Say thanks to them all.
—Mooji, Jamaican spiritual teacher

Forgive yourself for not being at peace. The moment you completely accept your non-peace . . . it is translated into peace. Anything you accept fully will get you there, will take you into peace. This is the miracle of surrender.
—Eckhart Tolle

May all that is unforgiven in you be released. May your fears yield their deepest tranquilities. May all that is unlived in you blossom into a future graced with love.
—John O'Donohue, To Bless the Space Between Us

*Love takes off the masks that we fear we cannot live without
and know we cannot live within. I use the word "love" here
not merely in the personal sense but as a state of being, or a
state of grace—not in the infantile American sense of being
made happy but in the tough and universal sense of quest
and daring and growth.*
—James Baldwin, The Fire Next Time

*Forgiveness is the fragrance that the violet sheds on the heel
that has crushed it.*
—Mark Twain

*Through me course wide rivers and in me rise tall moun-
tains. And beyond the thickets of my agitation and confusion
there stretch the wide plains of my peace and surrender. All
landscapes are within me. And there is room for everything.*
—Etty Hillesum, An Interrupted Life
and Letters from Westerbork

~ POEMS ~

"Do Not Be Ashamed"
by Wendell Berry

You will be walking some night
in the comfortable dark of your yard
and suddenly a great light will shine
round about you, and behind you
will be a wall you never saw before.
It will be clear to you suddenly
that you were about to escape,
and that you are guilty: you misread
the complex instructions, you are not

a member, you lost your card
or never had one. And you will know
that they have been there all along,
their eyes on your letters and books,
their hands in your pockets,
their ears wired to your bed.
Though you have done nothing shameful,
they will want you to be ashamed.
They will want you to kneel and weep
and say you should have been like them.
And once you say you are ashamed,
reading the page they hold out to you,
then such light as you have made
in your history will leave you.
They will no longer need to pursue you.
You will pursue them, begging forgiveness.
They will not forgive you.
There is no power against them.
It is only candor that is aloof from them,
only an inward clarity, unashamed,
that they cannot reach. Be ready.
When their light has picked you out
and their questions are asked, say to them:
"I am not ashamed." A sure horizon
will come around you. The heron will begin
his evening flight from the hilltop.

"Waiting"
by Raymond Carver

Left off the highway and
down the hill. At the
bottom, hang another left.
Keep bearing left. The road

will make a Y. Left again.
There's a creek on the left.
Keep going. Just before
the road ends, there'll be
another road. Take it
and no other. Otherwise,
your life will be ruined
forever. There's a log house
with a shake roof, on the left.
It's not that house. It's
the next house, just over
a rise. The house
where trees are laden with
fruit. Where phlox, forsythia,
and marigold grow. It's
the house where the woman
stands in the doorway
wearing the sun in her hair. The one
who's been waiting
all this time.
The woman who loves you.
The one who can say,
"What's kept you?"

"Allow"
by Danna Faulds

There is no controlling life.
Try corralling a lightning bolt,
containing a tornado. Dam a
stream and it will create a new
channel. Resist, and the tide
will sweep you off your feet.
Allow, and grace will carry

you to higher ground. The only
safety lies in letting it all in—
the wild and the weak; fear,
fantasies, failures and success.
When loss rips off the doors of
the heart, or sadness veils your
vision with despair, practice
becomes simply bearing the truth.
In the choice to let go of your
known way of being, the whole
world is revealed to your new eyes.

PERSONAL WRITINGS

Writing Topic:
Reflect on Forgiveness

Quote Prompt

You have no idea of the tremendous release and deep peace that comes from meeting yourself and your brothers totally without judgment. The strain of constant judgment is virtually impossible. It is curious that an ability so debilitating would be so deeply cherished.

—Helen Schucman, *A Course in Miracles*

In 1995, when I first began my work at the Chopra Center for Wellbeing, I was director of the teacher training program. One of my responsibilities was to organize the yearly certified instructor retreat. That year the site had already been selected: Crystal Mountain in Washington State, two hours from Seattle. Typical attendance was 150 instructors.

The retreat was in the summer. Connie volunteered to come along with me on the site visit in the fall, one of the many ways she supported me in my work. The retreat site was a ski resort that hosted other types of events in the summer. The accommodations were rustic at best but seemed to fit our needs.

For every retreat, volunteers were selected to help with various tasks. This was my first time I would be meeting the instructors and the volunteers. There was a ton of work to do to get prepared as well as on-site duties during the retreat. I had been assured that the volunteers were seasoned and ready to go.

A colleague and I flew to Seattle a couple of days before the retreat and drove the two hours on winding mountain roads up to Crystal Mountain. One of the big projects was compiling all the materials and assembling them in binders for the instructors. This was 1995 and computers and technology were not something common or portable. The day before the retreat we drove down to Seattle, found a Kinko's copy shop, made the final edits, and printed the manual pages. There was no paper with pre-punched holes. We carried and stacked boxes of the manuals in the trunk and back seat.

We drove back up the mountain after midnight. I took hours to hole punch and assemble the binders. Needless to say, we did not get much sleep. Somehow, the energy of the instructors arriving and welcoming them the next afternoon carried me through the next four days. The yoga instructor I lined up had backed out. Since I had finished a yoga teacher training program the year before, I got up at 5 am each day to teach the morning class. My head would hit the pillow after midnight.

We relied on the volunteers to do their jobs. During the retreat I noticed one volunteer, who I will call "Louise," whose mission it seemed was to hang out as close to Deepak as she could or gab with the instructors. I rarely saw her work. I felt myself getting angry and resentful toward her. I did not have time to oversee her activities. The hair on my neck stood up every time I passed her.

Wanting to give her the benefit of the doubt, I gave her one task, which was to line up the instructors to get their individual photo with Deepak. It was inconceivable to me, but Louise managed to mess this up. Perhaps my instructions were not clear, but my patience had worn thin. My revenge was telling the volunteer coordinator to never invite her back as a volunteer.

To my surprise, the next summer there she was again at the instructor retreat. Apparently, a volunteer had dropped out at the last minute and Louise was available. The retreat that summer was on the campus of University of California San Diego (UCSD), a large spread-out conglomeration of buildings and dormitories with five colleges.

We had planned the instructor retreat for three days leading into a seven-day seminar with both the instructors and other participants. There were 175 instructors at the retreat and 550 attendees signed up for the seminar. The logistics on campus were a bit complicated as we had to move from one end of the campus to the other after the instructor retreat finished to accommodate the larger group for the seminar.

During the retreat, I noticed Louise doing her typical routine of looking busy but not really doing anything. My resentment came back quickly. The last morning of the instructor retreat, we were told by the university organizers to have all the instructor luggage brought to a room which would be locked until they could move it for us later in the afternoon to the other side of the campus and the dormitories where everyone would be staying.

That meant over 200 pieces of luggage needed to be moved and stored in the room set aside for us. We accomplished that feat by 9 am. Midway through the morning, a university volunteer approached me and said the lock on the room where we had the luggage would not work and we needed to station someone there to guard the luggage. They would have someone stationed there until 1 pm, but we needed to have one of our volunteers cover from 1 to 4 pm.

I immediately thought of Louise. As suspected, she had weaseled her way into the tough assignment of being in the lecture hall when Deepak would speak from 1 to 4 pm as her volunteer task. When I told her what was needed, she grimaced. I did not give her an out. I gave her the keys to the van we had rented so she could get over to the room on the other side of campus to do the handoff by 1 pm.

Around 1:30 pm, she walked up to me in the lecture hall and promptly stated, "The luggage was gone." Trying to hide my disdain, I replied, "What? That is impossible." I was sure she had been to the wrong room. There were several large rooms near where the luggage had been stored. I checked, and she had the right room number. I was sure she had gone to the wrong room so I grabbed the van keys and said we would drive over together. I was furious. She was not going to get out of this assignment. Wasn't there a handoff? She said no. I was full of judgment and resentment. I thought, I will never forgive this woman if that luggage is gone.

Sure enough, when we got there the room was empty. We checked the other open rooms—no luggage. I had been told the luggage would be moved at 4 pm. There is nothing like a common enemy to bond people. I felt my walls come down as I knew she was my sole compatriot in getting this resolved.

As we shuttled from place to place on campus to find someone who knew what was going on and could help us, we got to know each other. I found out things about her background that made me appreciate her as a human being. She had lost her first husband and had raised her kids as a single mom. She had lived in San Francisco during the "summer of love" in the 1960s. I actually began to like her.

Two hours later, in the blistering heat of August, we had our answer. The university volunteers did not want to hang out in a room with luggage for three hours. They found another room somewhat of a distance from the original room and moved all the luggage there and locked the door. We had no knowledge of this and of course had no key. They had left long before Louise arrived at 1 pm.

The relief we felt was an understatement. There was no satisfactory feedback to be given to the university crew, as the ones who had made the decision to move the luggage without telling us were not there and the other twentysomethings truly did not care. Louise and I had bonded through this ordeal. By this time, we were laughing. My resentments, anger, and anticipatory need to forgive had dissolved.

For the next week of the seminar with 550 people, I could genuinely smile at Louise. We shared silent chuckles. I saw her rolling up her sleeves and pitching in. I am not sure what shifted. I think it was my attitude and energy toward her and hers toward me.

While this is not what I would consider a big life event requiring forgiveness work, it was something that taught me about building up anger and resentments. I needed to get to know Louise. I needed to connect with her and give her a fair chance to step up. I thanked her for her help. Like many themes in this book, they interweave with each other. In this case, connection, resentments, forgiveness, and gratitude were all part of the stew. *3/21/21*

Writing Topic:
Forgiveness Work

Quote Prompt

Forgiveness empties the past of its power to empty the present of its peace.

—L. R. Knost

When I review my life, there are very few forgiveness places left. I do not want to leave this world without doing this work. I get a twinge in my heart when I think about certain people and incidents in my life, but I do not believe that is because I still have aspects of them that I have not forgiven. I believe I have and I feel complete. I also have had things that I have forgiven myself for and I think those are complete as well.

One of the tricky parts for me with forgiveness revolves around a couple different people. I believe I have forgiven them in my heart, but it was not in person. I am curious about this and whether doing it in person or over the phone is a necessary step for complete forgiveness if the person is still alive. I have been told it is not.

Perhaps my thoughts about needing to do forgiveness work face to face is my curiosity as to what the other person's perspective is about what happened. I also hold out a hope that we would come to a deeper understanding than we ever thought possible.

One of the incidents involves a friend and former colleague who hurt me deeply. I sometimes wonder if we could ever be friends again and care about each other despite what happened and embrace our humanity together. I like the thought of that but am also afraid a conversation could go the wrong way and end up opening old wounds. I have forgiven her in my heart and I hope she has forgiven me. I have been at a standstill with whether to reach out to her for years. It is still a work in progress. 2021

Writing Topic:
Reflections on Divine Grace

All the major world religions, Buddhism, Judaism, Christianity, Hinduism, and Islam, have the concept of Grace or Divine Grace in their scriptures. The different translations and interpretations of these is way beyond the scope of what I am writing but it would be a worthy thing to explore.

What is important to me is where I started and why I wrote this book. I can find no other words to describe what happened to me that summer in my bedroom when I was twelve than Divine Grace.

The light I saw and felt was so beautiful and peaceful it defies any common vocabulary to define it. Many people who have had what they call near-death experiences have described it the same way. I have even read on occasion passages where the "voice" and "message" people have heard in such moments was very similar to what I heard. Encountering these same stories at random and unexpected times in my life always gives me goose bumps. The particular people and situations were vastly different than mine, but the same luminous light was felt and the same message was given.

It has never mattered to me if people question what I saw, felt, and heard. I know what I experienced and how it changed the course of my life for the better. When I think about it, I truly could bow down every day in gratitude for this Grace I was freely given. 2021

I am not sure I can capture Divine Grace any better than this poem by the mystic Sufi writer Hafiz:

Now is the time to know
That all that you do is sacred.

Now, why not consider
A lasting truce with yourself and God.

Now is the time to understand
That all your ideas of right and wrong

Were just a child's training wheels
To be laid aside

When you can finally live
With veracity
And love.

Hafiz is a divine envoy
Whom the Beloved
Has written a holy message upon.

My dear, please tell me,
Why do you still
Throw sticks at your heart
And God?

What is it in that sweet voice inside
That incites you to fear?

Now is the time for the world to know
That every thought and action is sacred

This is the time
For you to deeply compute the impossibility
That there is anything
But Grace.

Now is the season to know
That everything you do
Is sacred.

Haiku 2021

Paradox

you think it is for them
this business of forgiveness
think hard, think again

Holding It All

grace fell in my lap
from what God were you summoned
never lose hold of it

QUESTIONS TO CONTEMPLATE

❀ Have you forgiven yourself? How do you know?

❀ Have you had someone forgive you? How did it feel?

❀ Have you forgiven someone you did not want to forgive? How long did it take? Do you feel it is truly complete?

❀ Do you believe in the concept of Grace or Divine Grace? What does it mean to you?

Closing Thoughts

*May you listen to the voice within the beat even when
you are tired. When you feel yourself breaking down,
may you break open instead. May every experience in
your life be a door that opens your heart, expands your
understanding, and leads you to freedom. If you are
weary, may you be aroused by passion and purpose.
If you are blameful and bitter, may you be sweetened
by hope and humor. If you are frightened, may you be
emboldened by a big consciousness far wiser than your
fear. If you are lost, may you understand we are all lost,
and still we are guided—by Strange Angels and Sleeping
Giants, by our better and kinder natures, by the vibrant
voice within the beat. May you follow that voice, for This
is the way—the hero's journey, the life worth living, the
reason we are here.*

—Elizabeth Lesser

It is my fondest hope that you found something of value in this
book. I am humbled if you did. I hope that it made you think,
laugh, and cry and that you enjoyed it. I hope that it has changed
your life in some way for the better. Please know this book is Connie's and my gift to you. If you want to contribute in some form,
the best way to honor me is to give to a worthy cause in some way
you feel is most appropriate.

At this point in time, my desire is to give back and to give to
those I love and who have loved me. There are so many more sunsets I want to see, so many family gatherings I want to attend, and
so many more moments I want to enjoy. When those are gone, I

hope I have left the world a little better than when I came into it. I hope all my nieces and nephews and grandnieces and grandnephews live full, healthy, and love-filled lives. I won't see what the world becomes, but I do have faith that we are evolving and more people will begin to live from a place of higher consciousness. Our world is transforming and it can continue. Each of us has the choice to do our little part.

Copyright Permissions

Francine Sterle, "Hiking the Anza Borrego Desert After Surgery." Reprinted from *The Cancer Poetry Project*, ed. Karin B. Miller (Tasora Books, 2007) by permission of the author.

Excerpt from "Together" by Rosemerry Wahtola Trommer reprinted by permission of the author.

Chuang Tzu, "When the Shoe Fits." From *The Way of Chuang Tzu*, trans. Thomas Merton, copyright © 1965 by The Abbey of Gethsemani. Reprinted by permission of New Directions Publishing Corp.

Richard Wagamese, excerpt from *Embers* (Douglas and McIntyre, 2016) reprinted by permission of the publisher.

Margaret Wheatley, excerpt from "Turning to One Another." Reprinted from *Turning to One Another: Simple Conversations to Restore Hope to the Future*, 2nd edition (Berrett-Koehler Publishers, 2009) by permission of the publisher.

Miller Williams, "Compassion." Reprinted from *The Ways We Touch: Poems* (University of Illinois Press, 1997) by permission of the publisher.

Acknowledgments

This book would not be possible without the love and support of so many family, friends, and teachers. It is not possible to include everyone I want to thank, but please know that if you have received this book, you have inspired and helped me in some way on this journey.

To my large loving family, past and present: parents, Aggie and Hal; mother-in-law, Mom Villa; sister and brother-in law, Janine and Bob Obee; sisters-in-law and brothers-in-law, Olga O'Brien, Ramon Guillot, and Nini and Phil Epperson; niece and nephew, Courtney Delaunay and Perry Obee, and their spouses, Damien and Kimberly; cousin Tom Park and his wife, Gabby; cousin Moe Felix and his wife, one of my dearest friends, Susan Dunigan. You all have been there through it all and in times of great need, always there with a kind word, a meal, and ready to help.

To my friends who provided countless hours of encouragement and support, Cameron Plagens, Mary Ann Papageorge, Terri LeBeau, Arlene Kramer, Arleen Kagan, Laurie Wagner, Rob Fereau, Barb Shelli Sullivan, Karen Holhweck, Shivani Scheinman, Stuart Samuelson, Jill Mendlen, Gayle Cureton, Marilyn Obee, Pat Libby, Ann Fitzgerald, and Holly White Conklin.

To my Meditation Teacher Training peers and mentor, what a two-year journey into wisdom we undertook learning from each other and teaching together, Carolyn Woolley, Steve Scott, Robin Matuk, Monica LeMaster, Michelle LaRose, and our mentor, Jane Baraz.

To my Meditation Teacher Training practicum groups who stuck with me through thick and thin and helped me graduate, Barb Bush, Arleen Kagan, Laurie Wagner, Pat Libby, Barbara Britton, DeDe Smith, Duane MacGregor, Sandra Ulibari, Mary

Ann Papageorge, Arleen Kramer, Terri LeBeau, Irma Cota, and Laura Zweckbronner.

To my Healing Circles sisters from the Commonweal Cancer Help Program, Barb, Jeanne, Judy, Terry, Wendy, Cindy, Robin, Sheila and Amy. Your honesty and grit have inspired me. Your courage uplifted me every week. We share a bond that provided steady and loving wisdom when I needed it most.

To my writing teachers who gave me the tools, knowledge, and practice discipline that I needed and gave me the gift of knowing I could write. On many days, writing took me to places I never dreamed I could go. It was profoundly healing. There are not enough "thanks yous" for who you are and how you show up, Natalie Goldberg, Sharon Bray, Kadee Winters, Rob Wilder, and Dorotea Mendoza.

To the team who helped me publish this book: Susie Schaefer from Finish the Book Publishing for your professional and inspired project management and all the many tasks you tackled with grace, Amy Scott from Nomad Editorial for your beautiful and expert copy editing, Michelle White for your incredible design of this unconventional book and so expertly working with Connie's photos, and Caitlin O'Brien for your wealth of knowledge of getting permissions for quotes and poems and for doing it with such joy and aplomb. And to those permissions grantors who so generously waived or reduced any fees, my profound gratitude.

To the many wisdom teachers I have had the honor to study and sit with, your teachings have been among the most profound gifts of my life. Babaji (Hari Hari Ramji), I cannot express enough gratitude for being my teacher, for sharing your wisdom and welcoming me along with the Sonoma Ashram residents and many guests with an open heart into the sacred oasis you built. To Ram Dass, Jack Kornfield, Tara Brach, Carol Carnes, Debbie Ford, Michael Lerner, James Baraz, thank you all for the unique ways you have brought your teachings to shine in the world, inspiring me on my path of transformation.

To the Center for Spiritual Awakening in Pacific Grove and Pastor Bill Little, thank you for being one of the places we call our spiritual home. To the Nine Gates Mystery School leaders, Gay Luce and Deborah Jones, thank you for keeping this amazing program going over many years and for giving me my sacred vows to live by. To Rama Berch, my first yoga teacher, and Soraya Pereira, one of the finest yoga practitioners I have known and had the privilege to study with over 20 years.

To all the medical staff at University of California San Diego (UCSD) Moores Cancer Center and Koman Family Outpatient Pavilion who took care of me for seven years after my metastatic cancer diagnosis. Your care has been nothing short of phenomenal, competent, professional, and loving. To my oncologists, Barbara Parker, Rebecca Shatsky, and Shu Mei Kato, your dedication to me and to all your patients has been unwavering and exceptional. To my nurse practitioner, Kim Posada, and nurses Lynne Dillender and Shannon Moore, thank you for always being available and responsive, and for brightening my day. To all the nurses, pharmacy staff, radiologists, emergency room and hospital staff, aides, receptionists, schedulers, technicians, and host of others who serve cancer patients day in and day out at the UCSD clinics and hospitals: I hoped for good care but never expected the love and grace with which you all did your jobs, consistently outstanding, patient, and kind while juggling the needs of the many patients you serve.

A special thank you goes to Steven Kandel for helping Connie and me navigate the complicated maze of clinical trials and accompanying us to places like Duke University, MD Anderson, UCLA, Stanford University, and finally University of California San Francisco, where I was blessed to participate in a clinical trial during the 2020 COVID pandemic that enabled me to have eight more months with a good quality of life.

To those family members, friends, and teachers who faced the cancer journey before me and have passed on, I honor you, Denise

Walker, Victoria Felix, Sergio Salieri, Jane Barnett, David Dolan, Lupita Escobar, Chris Collwell, Janis Cohen, Tony Crocker-White, Debbie Ford, David Simon, and Lenore Lefer. To those I know who are on the cancer journey and who are survivors, I will not list your names here to respect and honor your privacy, but please know you have my deep respect for what you have gone through and are possibly going through right now. May the breakthroughs in cancer treatments come faster so you may all live long lives in health and love.

Finally, to Connie Villa, my partner in life and companion alongside me every step of the way on my cancer journey. You have lived the vow to stand beside me in sickness and in heath more than I could ever imagine. It was a gift and a delight to have your amazing photography be an integral part of this book, from the cover to the start of every chapter. Collaborating with you on this book project has brought me immense joy.

About the Photographer

Connie Villa's photography graces this book. She holds a degree in Environmental Design with emphasis in Architecture. In the early 1990s when the U.S. economy faced one of many recessions, her career as an intern architect came to an end and her professional life pivoted in a way that was completely different. Her world was altered by what became her second "temporary" career as a surgical assistant (yes, she went to school to become one). Working in the hospital operating room, Connie experienced a shift in priorities, faced with observations about what was essential and non-essential in life, and what made people genuinely happy: having a great family and good health.

It was during this time in 1995 that Connie and Nan met. Their genuine love and respect for one another and each other's family has been the core of their relationship spanning more than 25 years. Together they have enjoyed traveling, careers, watching grandnieces and grandnephews grow, and attending many family gatherings. Nan's acts of love, her kindness, generous nature, and strength of character are what Connie cherishes the most. She feels blessed to have Nan in her life.

For the last 20-plus years, Connie worked as a forensic architectural consultant, investigating construction-related defects. Connie's love of the natural environment ignited her passion for landscape and embarked on her nature photography journey in 2012 while she and Nan lived in Monterey, California.

Connie is a self-taught photographer. Her style is an expression of moments captured and details of tranquility that soothe the soul and inspire the spirit. She has studied at the Santa Fe Photographic Workshops with nature and architectural master photographers, and earned a certificate for landscape and travel photography at the New York Institute of Photography.

Connie's photography can be seen in collections at private homes and business offices. Her photography has been on exhibit in San Diego and New York. To see more of her work, please visit Cvillaphoto.com.

About the Author

Nan Johnson was blessed to have what she calls a moment of divine grace enter her life and awaken her when she was twelve years old. While she went on to complete college and graduate school and have a career in healthcare, her constant rudder was the search for the deeper meaning of life.

Nan believed a career in healthcare, serving people who were suffering in some way, complemented this quest for meaning. She dedicated over thirty years in the medical field in San Diego, California, at a variety of institutions from small private practices to large medical centers. Nan was the executive director for five years at the innovative, integrative health center of the Chopra Center for Wellbeing. For the last sixteen years of her career, Nan found her calling in hospice and end-of-life care.

Throughout her career Nan was in management and leadership positions, overseeing operations, business development, and clinical teams. At one juncture in the hospice field, she had over 250 staff reporting up to her through her managers and directors. She aspired to be a leader who inspired, provided clear direction, and upheld accountability and transparency. The hospice mission, patients, families, and her staff always came first.

While her roles and responsibilities kept her very busy, she was blessed to have a lifelong partner, Connie Villa, to share life with. Together over 25 years, they were legally married in 2014. They were fortunate to be able to take trips to see family and do what they loved most, being in nature. Their travel took them to the Grand Canyon for river rafting, the Amazon rainforest and Machu Picchu, Yosemite, Monterey, Big Sur, New Mexico, Vancouver, Hawaii, the Grand Tetons, and Idaho among many other sites. Many of the photos in this book are from their trips to these places.

Through it all, Nan had a lifelong passion to explore spirituality in its various forms and take workshops and retreats with different wisdom teachers. She did this over three decades. Her book, *Legacy of Love*, is a culmination of what she has learned along the way. She always had a desire to write books, and even though she did not get to write as many as she had hoped, there has been no better way to share some of herself and what she has learned than writing this book for you.

www.ingramcontent.com/pod-product-compliance
Lightning Source LLC
Chambersburg PA
CBHW040853120626
46551CB00001B/6